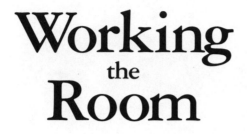

Working
the
Room

Working
the
Room

**HOW TO MOVE PEOPLE TO ACTION THROUGH
AUDIENCE-CENTERED SPEAKING**

Nick Morgan

HARVARD BUSINESS SCHOOL PRESS

Boston, Massachusetts

Library of Congress Cataloging-in-Publication Data

Morgan, Nick.
    Working the room : how to move people to action through
audience-centered speaking / Nick Morgan.
        p. cm.
      ISBN 1-57851-819-9 (alk. paper)
  1. Public speaking. I. Title.
      PN4129.15.M67 2003
      808.5'1--dc21

                                2002154824

To Nikki

CONTENTS

ACKNOWLEDGMENTS IX

INTRODUCTION

The Only Reason to Give a Speech
Is to Change the World   1

PART I   HISTORY AND OVERVIEW

CHAPTER 1

How Did We Get Here?   11

CHAPTER 2

What to Do? The Audience-Centered
Presentation Process   21

PART II   PREPARING THE CONTENT

CHAPTER 3

Understand the Audience   37

CHAPTER 4

Craft the Elevator Speech   47

CHAPTER 5

Pick the Level of Need   51

viii Contents

CHAPTER 6

Find the Story   61

CHAPTER 7

Structure the Content   73

CHAPTER 8

Make the Journey   85

CHAPTER 9

Involve the Audience   97

PART III   REHEARSING THE PRESENTATION

CHAPTER 10

Search for the Truth   113

CHAPTER 11

Choreograph the Kinesthetics   125

CHAPTER 12

Pay Attention to What Your Audience Needs   137

CHAPTER 13

Conquer Your Fear   143

CHAPTER 14

Get Technical   153

PART IV   STAND AND DELIVER

CHAPTER 15

The Audience-Centered Speech   171

CHAPTER 16

Listen to Your Audience   181

CHAPTER 17

Audience-Centered Speaking for All Occasions   199

CONCLUSION

The Secret of Charisma   225

ABOUT THE AUTHOR   229

ACKNOWLEDGMENTS

My interest in public speaking began in graduate school debating rhetorical points with Professor E. D. Hirsch, and for his tutelage and that of the many other professors and fellow students at the University of Virginia, I am grateful.

I first learned speechwriting from Chief of Staff David McCloud, Press Secretary George Stoddart, and Governor Charles S. Robb of Virginia. Their teaching was brisk and professional and I will always be in their debt.

From my students at Princeton University, the University of Virginia, and Lehigh University I learned much, and with their help and constant feedback first developed many of the principles in this book. They have my affection and thanks always. In particular, Andrew Boer has helped me as much as I have helped him over the years. Thanks to Andy and the family. Thanks also to Alex Kinnier, who listened to an early version of these ideas and put them brilliantly into practice.

It is chiefly, though, to my clients at Gemini Consulting, Index, and many other companies, that thanks must go for helping me to hone the insights contained herein. In particular, the people of Research Services have shared my passion for getting public speaking right, and they have tried out many of these ideas with faith and enthusiasm. Thanks, Richard, for first hiring me and then arguing with me so eloquently over the years. Thanks, Nikki, David, Richard, Espen, Tony, Paul, Tony, Alex, Andy, Anne, Anna, Carole, Cher, Chris, Donal, Chris, Doug, Francis, James, Jane, Guy, Jon, Keri, Kate, Keren, Richard, Lem, Linda, Lyn, Mary, Mel, Piet, Patrick, Tudor, Ian, and Victoria.

The people of Harvard Business School Publishing have inspired me, taught me, helped me, worked with me, and pushed me always to do better. Thanks, Walter, for bringing me on board. Thanks to the Newsletters and Conferences Group past and present, whose hard work has made it possible for me to get a newsletter out and write a book and consult with clients at the same time. Thanks to the Harvard ManageMentor team for its energy and creativity. Thanks of course to the Press folks, and my editor, Jeff Kehoe, for patiently and expertly seeing this book through to publication. Thanks to the *Harvard Business Review* for publishing "The Kinesthetic Speaker," in which the seed of this book first began to sprout. And thanks to my agent, Jim Levine, for spotting the promise contained therein.

Thanks to Greg and Seth of Public Words. Thanks are also due to fellow journeymen Ruth Mott, Richard Greene, and Jeff Ansell.

Finally, thanks to my extended families for all their support, love, and forgiveness. Thanks to Marjie. And thanks to Sarah and Eric for patiently hearing many of these thoughts over and over again as they were growing up. For them, the rules of good public speaking are as simple and obvious as Saturday morning waffles.

The Only Reason to Give a Speech Is to Change the World

THE ONLY REASON TO GIVE A SPEECH IS to change the world. An old friend of mine, a speechwriter, used to say that to me. He meant it as a challenge. It was his way of saying that, if you're going to take all the trouble to prepare and deliver a speech, make it worthwhile. Change the world.

Otherwise, why bother? Preparing speeches, giving speeches, and listening to speeches—each of these activities is fraught with peril. The opportunities for failure are many, and for success correspondingly few. An oft-quoted study suggests that executives would rather die than speak. Of all their fears, public speaking is number one, and death comes much further down the list, just before nuclear war. That must explain why they often put off the task of preparing speeches to the last minute—or give the task to someone else.

If speechmaking is hard work for presenters, it's also hard work for their audiences. Most business presentations are dreadful—boring, platitudinous, and delivered with a compelling lack of enthusiasm. People don't remember much of what they learn from speeches—something on the order of 10 percent to 30 percent. With some business talks I've attended, that failure rate must be close to 100 percent. How many presentations have you sat through where your mind started wandering a few minutes into the talk and never really came back? Where you surreptitiously picked up your date book and started planning your calendar for the next millennium or two? Where you ended up more familiar with the number of acoustic tiles in the ceiling than the number of points in the outline of the speech?

So why do we bother? We bother giving speeches because of the opportunities they offer presenters with passion and a cause. There is something profound about gathering a group of people together in a hall and giving them the full force of your ideas presented "live and in person." There is something essential about the intellectual, emotional, and physical connections a good speaker can make with an audience, something that cannot happen on the printed page. There is something powerful about the chemistry that happens in the moment of contact that no other medium can reproduce.

It's what I call the *kinesthetic connection*. It's something I've observed in more than seventeen years of teaching and coaching public speaking. When it happens, it's powerful. When it's missing, everyone feels it—even the hapless speaker. Helping you find that connection, which is at the heart of giving what I call the *audience-centered presentation,* is what this book is all about.

The need to speak is never-ending.

We still need speeches. We need them to move audiences to action. People may learn to believe in your expertise from the printed page. But they will only be moved to action if they come to trust you from hearing and seeing you offer a solution to a problem they have. That kind of trust is visceral as well as intellectual and emotional, and it only comes from presence.

From the audience's point of view, we still need to validate our impulse to action by seeing our champions, to test the sense of their messages and the integrity of their beings. Partly, we're reading their nonverbal messages, those gestures and habits that we learn to interpret unconsciously for the most part, the ones that tell us something about the credibility and courage of the presenter. Partly, we're testing to see if they can structure and present their ideas coherently in real time, abilities that tell us about how articulate and organized they are. And partly, we're watching to see if we can find some sense of common humanity in the speaker, in order to make common cause with that speaker's passion.

When Roger Mudd asked Ted Kennedy, on *60 Minutes* in 1980, why he wanted to be president, Senator Kennedy famously fumbled the answer. Millions of Americans watched Kennedy at close hand, thanks to the eye of the camera, and judged his incoherent, rambling answer to lack credibility. The campaign was over almost before it began. Kennedy had changed the world— not in the way he intended, perhaps, but inescapably and irretrievably nonetheless. Potential backers slunk away from the Kennedy camp. Potential workers joined other campaigns. Potential voters resolved to find another candidate. And all of that happened through the faux-familiarity of television. Imagine how much more devastating it would have been in person.

Does changing the world seem like a daunting challenge? There's good news buried in the challenge. With a powerful, *audience-centered* presentation, *you can change the world*. And that goes whether you're talking to a small group of employees or colleagues—or a keynote audience of thousands. The principles are the same.

And there's more good news to come: Regardless of how good you are now, you can learn how to give a better speech, one that makes a kinesthetic connection with your listeners. One that creates a sense of trust in you and moves them to action.

You need to listen to your audience.

At the heart of this connection lies a counterintuitive truth: *The secret to forming a strong bond between you and the people in the audience is to listen to them—from the very beginning.*

Wait a minute, you say. I'm the one that has to do the talking. How can I listen to them? And what do you mean by kinesthetic? You've already used that word twice.

The answers to these questions are related. Let's take the easy one first. *Kinesthetic* means being aware of the position and movement of the body in space. And to listen to the audience, you need to listen (and to show you're listening) with your whole body. To give a simple example, consider the nervous executive in front of the shareholders for an annual meeting. He has some less-than-spectacular numbers to report, and everyone knows it. He's prepared for the worst. He begins his talk with a curt, "Good morning," arms folded, staring tensely over the audience members' heads, looking into the middle distance, trying not to acknowledge the anger he sees in front of him. He immediately launches into a defensive talk aimed at minimizing the damage and second-guessing what the audience might ask him.

Not a pretty picture. Contrast that with a different executive in a similar pickle. She knows the meeting is going to be tough, but she's ready. She stands up in front of the shareholders, smiles, and asks, "How are you?" Her arms are comfortably open at her sides. And she waits for a couple of seconds, making eye contact with at least one of the audience members on the right hand side of the room. Then she asks, no longer smiling, raising her eyebrows to invite response, "Are you angry about last year's numbers? [*Pause. Looking at someone else, on the left, now.*] You have every right to be. We're as disappointed as you are. Let's talk about them. What's on your mind?"

Not many chief executives would have the guts, frankly, to take the second approach. But which company would you rather hold stock in?

The second executive is well on the way to giving an audience-centered speech. She's going to find kinesthetic moments to connect with her audience, and she's begun by actually listening to them—reading their entire range of responses, including the nonverbal—from the start.

Indeed, in this simplified example, the key to success is in making those rhetorical questions real. When you ask, "How are you?" of an audience, wait to see how some members of that audience actually are. Don't continue until you've learned the answer, either verbally or nonverbally. It's a small but vital way to begin an audience-centered talk. Success in public speaking is made up of myriad little moments of connection like that.

And one big thing: charisma. That's the magic quality, isn't it? The one that everyone craves. And yet charisma doesn't come from doing something difficult or esoteric that it takes years to master (and lots of expensive advice from speech coaches like me). We know now, thanks to the communications research of the last thirty years, what charisma is. Quite simply, it's *expressiveness*. Expressiveness is the willingness to be open to your audience, both verbally and nonverbally. To show how you feel about your subject. To get past nervousness and self-consciousness and get to the stuff that you care about, and *give that to the audience*. That's why they call it "*giving* a speech." If you can unlock your own passion about the subject, and give that to the audience, you will be charismatic. The audience will not be able to take its eyes off you.

And so we're back to audience-centered speaking, and kinesthetics. The only reason to give a speech is to change the world. You accomplish that by moving your audience to action. To do that, you have to be willing to listen to the audience, and to give it your passion. To get to that happy state, you need to find kinesthetic connections with the audience.

That's audience-centered speaking in a paragraph. It's as simple as that.

And lest you think that when I say "changing the world" I'm only talking about the big speeches (the ones that CEOs give to shareholders, for example) understand that I'm talking about *every speech ever given.* The principles and practical tools in this book (and we will get to the practical part soon) apply to all public speaking, whether to five thousand people or five, for a grand public occasion or simply a regular meeting to report on third quarter numbers. After all, if you give a brilliant, inspiring, audience-centered presentation about those third quarter numbers, you will change the attitudes of your team in the room with you. And if you change their attitudes, you just might change their behavior. And if you change their behavior, you've changed the world in the only way that counts.

So let's get started. We're going to range over a good deal of ground, and I'm going to give a great deal of practical advice for beginners and experts alike. You should feel free to apply those parts of the book that are most directly useful to you. The general principles apply to all kinds of speeches, as I've said, but you may not need to rehearse, for example, in some of the ways I've suggested. It's up to you. What follows is a book, not a speech, but nonetheless I would like it to be as audience-centered as possible. You're going to learn how to work the room by reading this book, and to do that effectively you need to develop an approach that is your own.

In part I, you'll learn, through a brief history of public speaking, why it works the way it does, and why most of modern speech making is so bad. Then, I'll introduce you to the audience-centered approach that will enable you to rise above the ordinary level of presentations and presenters.

In part II, you'll learn how to prepare the content. Most speech coaches will tell you to focus on your clothing or your smile. But people do go to presentations to hear content first, and it's essential to get it right. You need to deliver your talk in a way that respects the audience's need to make a decision about the argument you're presenting to them. Accordingly, I walk you through a process that begins with understanding the audience, and crafting an elevator speech that fits that audience. Then we address the psychological needs of the audience, find a story that fits the event, structure the content in a way that makes sense to your listeners, plan the journey that we're going to take that audience on, and figure out how to get them involved in the most dynamic way.

In part III, we'll talk about how to rehearse the presentation you've developed. I'll show you how to rehearse certain aspects of your speech to find its truth. I talk about how to choreograph your speech kinesthetically, so that you use your body to reinforce your message rather than detract from it, as most speakers do. We'll focus also on what the audience needs in terms of kinesthetic, aural, and visual learning, and we'll close with some help for the very nervous and some technical information.

Finally, in part IV, I'll take you through the day of delivery itself, and give you some warm-up tips to help you cope with nerves and maximize your performance. We'll talk about how to put the energy of the audience to work for you. And I'll wrap up the section with a chapter on a variety of specific public-speaking issues, such as question-and-answer sessions, the media, videoconferencing, and the like. By the time you've worked your way through the book, you should be prepared for most public-speaking challenges, and you should have a good grounding in audience-centered speaking.

A brief note on terminology: Many businesspeople make a strong distinction between a "speech" and a "presentation." The former is a big deal to a lot of people, and the latter is something more informal, perhaps a talk in front of colleagues or employees. Part of the argument of this book is that there is no real distinction between the two. The same principles apply no matter how many people you're talking to. In fact, it's easier to apply these principles to small groups than large. Thus I will use the two terms, speech and presentation, interchangeably.

Remember

- The only reason to give a speech is to change the world.

- Effective speeches move their audiences to action.

- Effective speakers listen to their audiences.

- Charisma comes from the ability to be emotionally expressive.

- To deliver a successful speech, find kinesthetic connections with the audience.

PART I

History and Overview

CHAPTER 1

How Did We Get Here?

'LL BEGIN WITH A BRIEF HISTORY OF HOW we got to the rather sorry state of public speeches and presentations we find ourselves in today. Trust me; it's important to help you understand why kinesthetic speaking is so vital to success in the modern, post-television era.

The Ancient Greeks invented public speaking because they had to.

The idea that ordinary people should stand up and deliver public presentations began with the Ancient Greeks. In their legal system, the opposing sides were expected to speak for themselves in court. Around this dire necessity, a whole lore of public-speaking tips and advice developed. Soon enough, the plaintiffs and defendants began to hire expert *rhetors* (think lawyer) to speak for them. The field of rhetoric grew up in response to this need for private citizens and their representatives to speak clearly, cogently, and powerfully in public settings where a lot was at stake.

At the same time, political figures found the need to speak on matters of public moment, much as they do today. Both these strands of public speaking led to the creation of a good deal of advice on how to give great presentations, and some classic speech examples. Much of this body of rhetorical knowledge is still useful today. The Greeks have left us with excellent, detailed advice on how to recognize faulty arguments, how to create elegant *tropes*, or turns of phrase that will move listeners, and how to structure a persuasive speech that works in front of an audience.

In addition, they gave some very practical advice on how to deliver a speech. Since we have no direct knowledge of what the best Greek speakers actually sounded or looked like, the practical advice is limited to a few concepts and stories.

Demosthenes, for example, was a noted Greek public orator who began with what must have been sloppy pronunciation or perhaps a speech impediment. He practiced his speeches on the beach when no one else was around, taking smooth pebbles from the sand and putting them in his mouth. Once he could speak clearly with pebbles, he removed them and found that he quickly became known for the clarity of his delivery.

That technique has come down to us today, and there are still speech coaches who recommend that their "mush-mouthed" students practice their speeches holding a pencil between their teeth or the like. It remains a good idea for people who have difficulty enunciating clearly in public settings. But, of course, it's not the whole story, as we shall see. Far more confusion is generated by speakers whose verbal and nonverbal communications are inconsistent, or who present their material in confusing and poorly structured ways, first annoying and then alienating their audiences.

To succeed in a presentation, you have to reach your audience with both head and heart.

Public speaking is a mixed genre of human activity. It involves both intellectual and emotional content. It demands both clear thinking and good technique. It uses both the brain and the body. Most important, it is both prepared and given—it exists in both theory and practice. You can't "think" a speech. For it to be a speech you must have an audience, and you must give that audience the presentation. The Greeks understood this. Their analysis of what it takes to be a great speaker pays attention to both story structure and performance in the broadest sense. What follows will use many of their insights, still powerful two thousand years on.

Thus, we can pass relatively quickly over most of the ensuing two thousand years of rhetorical history and come to the modern era. In the Renaissance and after, the ancient Greek models were considered the acme of public speaking and followed closely. Since much of the university curriculum was based on the Greeks and the Romans, when it wasn't based on the Bible, there was little innovation in public rhetoric. Demosthenes' name, for example, was still a byword for excellence in delivery well into the first half of the twentieth century.

Through the Victorian era, public speaking drew inspiration from the ancients.

The Victorian enthusiasm for most things classical kept Greek and Roman rhetoric at the forefront of the field of public speaking throughout the period. While there was rapid change on many other fronts, from agriculture to transportation, in presentations the Victorians were tradition-bound. By 1900, for instance, little had changed in the basic understanding of public oratory since the Greeks except that a collection of conventional gestures, designed to convey emotion, had slowly evolved and become codified in self-help books for speakers and actors, especially during the eighteenth and nineteenth centuries. No doubt the Greeks had gestures of their own; it's just that we have no clear record of what they were.

But we do have a record of some of the gestures that were thought appropriate since the mid-1700s. Indeed, some of them are still used in a modified, naturalized form today. When you see someone put his hands in front of his mouth in shock or horror, for example, that is the modern version of a gesture conveying horror that has been around since at least the Victorian era, and probably much longer.

These gestures were important because of how speeches were delivered until the advent of radio and television in the mid-twentieth century. It's important to understand that public speaking was a form of mass entertainment. Most speeches were delivered without amplification to audiences in large halls or outdoors. As a result, a style of speaking developed that involved grand rhetoric, big, dramatic gestures, and voice projection. Most speakers followed the Greek models for how to structure a speech, and those speeches often lasted for several hours.

Lincoln's Gettysburg Address was a now-famous exception. The speech was barely noticed in the press reports that followed. It was over so quickly that, legend has it, the photographer didn't even have time to get a picture. He was still setting up his camera when Lincoln sat down, already finished. Most of the press focused instead on the long speech by Edward Everett that followed Lincoln's. Everett spoke for two hours, an acceptable length for a funeral oration of the day. He used as his model Pericles' funeral oration on the death of the Athenian soldiers who fell during the Peloponnesian War against Sparta, which had become over the years the accepted paradigm for all funeral orations.

Like much that was excellent about the Ancient Greeks and

Romans, the formal generic demands of the funeral oration were largely forgotten after World War II—until President Ronald Reagan reinvented the genre for his brilliant speech on the Challenger disaster in 1986.

Typical of nineteenth-century oration too was William Jennings Bryan's famous "cross of gold" speech, which he delivered more than six hundred times around the country to large, enthusiastic crowds in his failed presidential campaign of 1896. Bryan was arguing for a combined gold- and silver-based monetary system and against a gold standard—a relatively arcane economic argument that pitted the common people against the moneyed interests of the day. Bryan's voice thundered and his arms flailed in grand style; he could ignite a crowd of two thousand, making his voice heard with careful breathing and other projection techniques honed over a lifetime of public oratory.

But the physical techniques Bryan employed to reach such a large crowd unamplified are not the only things that are different than today. Our ideas about content have also changed. It's worth looking briefly at the very end of Bryan's several-hour speech to understand the differences.

It is the issue of 1776 over again. Our ancestors, when but three millions in number, had the courage to declare their political independence of every other nation; shall we, their descendants, when we have grown to seventy millions, declare that we are less independent than our forefathers? No, my friends, that will never be the verdict of our people. Therefore, we care not upon what lines the battle is fought. If they dare to come out in the open field and defend the gold standard as a good thing, we will fight them to the uttermost. Having behind us the producing masses of this nation and the world, supported by the commercial interests, the laboring interests, and the toilers everywhere, we will answer their demand for a gold standard by saying to them, you shall not press down upon the brow of labor this crown of thorns; you shall not crucify mankind upon a cross of gold.

Try to imagine a crowd of two thousand farmers leaping to their feet, roaring approval for several minutes, and you'll have some idea of the effect Bryan's speech had everywhere he went. How does the rhetoric seem to your ear and eye? Overly formal? A bit pompous? Note how it is designed to spread out the key concepts with enough words in between to get the thought out. It simply took the sound waves of Bryan's voice a little while to travel out to two thousand people and be heard and understood. Hence, when Bryan asks a rhetorical question ("shall we, their descendants . . . declare that we are less independent . . . ?") he is careful to answer it, so that no one in the audience is in any doubt about the correct response. Nowadays, answering an obviously rhetorical question like that would sound excessively pompous.

Note also how Bryan ends most of his sentences with strong words that can be shouted or projected on an "up" note. Today, we're more casual, but back then, the first need was to be heard. If your voice trails off, people will lose the last few words, and then often the sense of the whole phrase. That's why Bryan says, "we care not upon what lines the battle is fought." To our ears, the phrasing is old-fashioned, but for Bryan, the key words ("care not," "lines," "battle," "fought") are spaced appropriately and end with a strong verb that ties the whole phrase together. It's phrasing appropriate for shouted oratory. Moreover, it's composed for the most part of simple, short words that have wide, powerful meanings. Bryan well understood his audience—its strengths and its limitations.

In the twentieth century, technology changed public speaking permanently and profoundly.

Since the advent of amplified sound and later television, the genre of public speaking has changed enormously. Oratory evolved from a shouted genre to a spoken one. Then, beginning in the 1950s, when we took to watching our public discussions on television, public speaking became an *intimate* genre.

Therein lies the dilemma for most speakers today. Instead of watching a speaker address us from a distant stage, we invited Walter Cronkite and a host of imitators into our homes. With the television screen framing his head and shoulders, Cronkite appeared to be talking to us from a few feet away, within a space we usually reserve for chat about fairly personal matters with people we trust. The close personal contact (or the illusion of it, at least) made us feel connected to Cronkite and other television figures. They became implicitly trustworthy in our minds.

In this seemingly intimate space created by television, the old-fashioned approach to the delivery of public presentations—the large gestures, the sweeping phrases, the carefully spaced concepts—was obviously out of place. What we needed instead, and what we gradually got, was the personal conversation appropriate to this cozy environment. Unfortunately, we also forgot a good deal of what remains profound about the Greeks' understanding of public rhetoric, especially its content and structure, in our need to become modern. Slowly, the illusion of physical closeness conveyed by television created in all audiences an expectation of intimacy, both spatial and emotional, from a speaker.

This phenomenon is why we all have the slightly eerie feeling that we know our celebrities. It's because we have let them into our living rooms, and more important, our personal space. We watch them talk to us conversationally from a few feet away, seemingly in our kitchens, our living rooms, our family rooms, our bedrooms.

Today we have a mismatch between public-speaking custom and audience expectations.

Most public oratory—especially business speeches and presentations—has never entirely caught up with the audience's changed expectations. Our speaking styles have indeed become more conversational, but speakers in public spaces haven't learned to deliver the physical closeness that mirrors the linguistic closeness on television.

Moreover, the candid personal disclosure that we have grown to expect when we are seemingly so close to a televised speaker hasn't become part of public presentations for the most part—especially, again, in business presentations. After all, no self-respecting CEO is about to pattern his or her presentations after the intimacy of Oprah.

We're left today with some clumsy disparities in public oratory. There is the disjunction between the trappings of traditional public speaking—the podium, the large auditorium, the stage, the lighting—and a style of discourse that is now more conversational than declamatory. Even more significant, a yawning gap exists between an audience's ingrained expectations, shaped by a half-century of watching television, and the behavior of most business, educational, and governmental speakers. Even in the relatively intimate setting of a small conference room, the typical speaker is kinesthetically disconnected, though he or she isn't physically distanced from the audience. Instead of occasionally moving toward the audience to establish a personal connection, speakers usually move back and forth between the podium or projector and the screen in a weirdly hypnotic, solipsistic form of what could be called presentational dance. They might as well be talking to themselves. The audience sits watching in suspended animation through this faux-kinesthetic routine until the question-and-answer session at the end, when attendees are offered a brief chance to move and perhaps to speak.

Also, while the speaker's tone may be more conversational these days, the audience's intuitive expectation of a personal message delivered at close range usually goes unfulfilled. With the lights turned low so that slides can be seen, with little kinesthetic stimulation from the speaker, and with little opportunity for the audience to respond in turn, the crowd will gradually tune out. The overall, if unintended, effect is to disconnect the speaker from the message, the message from the audience, and the audience from action—the main reason for the oratorical effort in the first place.

In a word, it's boring. And it's boring because medium, style, and message no longer connect. We expect intimacy, like what we see on television, and instead we get poorly structured, unemotional corporate-speak.

Indeed, given the skewed evolution of public-speaking content and delivery against the backdrop of the enforced intimacy of modern media, the wonder is that speeches are ever interesting at all. The few speeches that do manage to ignite an audience's passion are exceptions to a dismal rule of mediocrity.

How can we change this sorry dynamic? By learning (from, first of all, the Greeks) to develop content that is appropriate to the aural genre of the presentation, by rehearsing it to find the kinesthetic moments—the opportunities for connection with the audience—and by learning how to deliver it in a kinesthetic style that is compelling for audiences today. By developing, in short, the audience-centered rhetoric needed for the twenty-first century.

Remember

- The Ancient Greeks invented public speaking out of a need to argue legal cases.

- Public speaking is a mixed genre of human activity—it involves both head and heart, theory and practice, understanding and performance.

- Through the Victorian era, public speaking drew inspiration from the ancients.

- In the twentieth century, technology, including radio and television, changed public speaking permanently and profoundly.

- Today we have a mismatch between public-speaking custom and audience expectation.

- We need a new rhetoric for the twenty-first century—an audience-centered rhetoric.

CHAPTER 2

What to Do?
The Audience-Centered
Presentation Process

W E ENDED CHAPTER 1 WITH A
call for an audience-centered rhetoric for the twenty-first century,
one that would respect the audience's need to come to a decision
in real time. We'll begin at the most important place: the content.

How do you shape the content of an audience-centered speech?
Much that is useful has been lost in our evolution to casual, conversational speakers. Public speaking must be more than merely
conversation on your hind legs. Have you ever listened hard to a
real conversation between two other people? If you're not looking
directly at both parties, it can be almost impossible to follow.

Conversations are full of stops and starts, incomplete thoughts and utterances, and references to body language such as gestures, facial expressions, and what the nonverbal communications researchers call *emblems*, or gestures that have specific coded meaning in particular cultures. It's a messy business.

Public speaking is structured conversation.

Content must be given to the audience in a way that recognizes the audience's need to absorb information through an aural genre with limited opportunities for feedback of the kind that conversation provides. That is not to say that there is no feedback in public speaking—there's actually plenty. But because most public speaking is more or less scripted, the speaker is limited in the amount of attention he can give to feedback, and limited in the ways in which he can respond.

Think of a presentation as a train journey. It's linear—on a particular track—unlike conversation. You don't get the opportunity to stop the train very often. If you get off the train, you quickly get left behind. So you don't get the next idea, because you're floundering around trying to get back on the train.

Thus, the content needs to proceed logically, in complete thoughts, with stops along the way for the audience to check its comprehension.

Listening is exhausting work, and people don't retain much of what they hear. How can you improve on the low retention rate? First, it's a matter of structuring the content so that it is organized and delivered the way the audience needs to hear it.

Second, it's a matter of ruthless focus. Think in terms of getting one idea across to the audience; if your audience will only remember one thing, what would you tell them? Throw everything else away.

Third, what is your emotional content? You should give just as much thought to preparing an emotional story line as an intellectual one.

Take your audience on a journey from *why* to *how*.

We'll get into more detail later, but for now, imagine that your speech will take the audience on a journey. The audience comes into a talk wanting to have a key question answered: Why? Why am I here? Why is this topic important? Why should I pay attention to the speaker for the next hour or so?

This is a key difference between conversation and public speaking. People engage in conversation by and large for mutual pleasure, the exchange of information, or storytelling—or some mix of the three. You don't need to answer the "Why?" question, typically, for your friend to talk with you.

But public speaking is different. You need to orient the audience and prepare the way for the information you have to give them. To do that, you need to set them at ease and give them a context for your presentation. Sometimes a good introduction can do some of that work, but most of it still must be done by the speaker.

Once you've answered the "Why?" question, you take your audience on the journey that reveals your answer. If you've done your job well, the audience will be asking "How?" by the end of the talk. How do I implement this idea? How do I take this vision and make it my own? And perhaps the most important one, as we'll see: How do I get started right now?

Move the audience from why *to* how. That's your goal. That's a successful speech, whether to five people, or fifty, or five thousand.

Don't tell them all you know.

The audience provisionally grants you authority by becoming an audience—sitting down and preparing to listen to you. The audience bestows a mantle of trust and credibility upon you at the beginning of a speech. It's up to you to wear it successfully. Don't betray that trust. Stick to the point, and make it possible for your audience to continue to allow you to be its expert.

The essence of successful public speaking is focus—focusing on the emotional content, focusing on the one key idea you want to get across, and focusing on the audience.

Connect with your audience by telling them stories.

Recent research into the workings of the brain suggests something that we all know intuitively: We make sense of our world by piecing together stories. In fact, from the cradle on up, we deduce cause and effect by creating primitive stories about what we see around us. Sitting in a high chair, we push over the cup of milk and watch in delight and fascination as the white liquid runs over the tray and down to the floor. Then the adults around us make a lot of noise and rush around cleaning things up. What a story!

From there, we develop increasingly sophisticated stories to explain how the world around us works. And we learn the stories our society tells us as a way of further understanding the apparent chaos of modern life.

Good public speaking connects with each individual audience member's need to understand what's being said in terms of stories. Think of the journey you're going to take your audience on (the one from why to how) as a kind of story. Your audience will understand it better if it has all the parts of a good story—a strong protagonist, a clear dilemma for him or her to work on, and a happy ending.

In Western society, we have some basic stories that all of us learn at a very early age and that are reinforced by virtually endless repetition throughout our lives. The most fundamental is the Quest, but there are four others that we also have woven into our deepest cultural understandings. If you can weave some of the elements of a good Quest story, or one of the other fundamental ones, into your presentation, your audience will "get" the idea you're trying to get across much more quickly and much more powerfully. In addition, the likelihood that they'll remember what you have to say will go up enormously. I'll say more about these stories in chapter 6.

Give your speech to the members of the audience by allowing them to become active.

Audiences are filled by and large with people who like to be active. They think of themselves as decision makers. For a good deal of your presentation, you're asking these active decision makers to be passive. A good speech therefore describes a journey not only from why to how, but also from passive to active.

This is especially true of smaller audiences and more casual occasions—the typical business fare of ten or twenty people listening to a leader bring them up to date or exhort them to sell more widgets. Larger audiences in more formal occasions probably expect to be entertained (well or badly) rather than moved to action.

Far too many speakers, in a misguided desire to maintain control of what often seems like a potentially chaotic situation, refuse to "give" the speech to the audience. Instead, they hold on to it, keeping it for themselves. The result is at best an informative lecture. It is not a speech that moves people to action; it cannot therefore be a persuasive speech, except in the very limited sense that it could persuade the audience that the speaker is a learned person.

If you want to move your audience, you must learn to "give" the speech to them. Allow them full participation. Let them act upon your ideas. Move them from passive to active.

The single most important thing you can do to prepare a speech is to rehearse.

First of all, let me say that no matter how much I preach the virtues of rehearsal, some of those reading this book will nonetheless not do it. Why? On the face of it, it seems inconceivable that an executive could approach something as potentially important as a public presentation—even an "everyday" one—without extensive rehearsal. And yet many do. In my seventeen years of preparing, teaching, and coaching presentations and public speeches ranging from client sales pitches to campaign kick-offs and State of the Union addresses, I have seen more speeches fail from lack of rehearsal than any other single problem.

Do you think an internal speech to your staff doesn't "count"? Then you've just lost an opportunity to change the world in the way that is most important to you. You have the most effect on the world closest to home, after all.

I've heard all the excuses, from "it's just a little throwaway" to "if I rehearse I lose my spontaneity." If a presentation is worth giving, it's worth rehearsing at least once. If it's not, then why would you be giving it?

Fundamentally, people avoid rehearsal because speech making is fraught with anxiety, and executives, politicians, and educational leaders feel about anxiety the way just about everyone else does: They try to avoid it. So, believe it or not, they put off the anxiety, greatly compounding the risk that the actual performance will be less than optimal, rather than face the worst of it during rehearsal.

Don't do it. Please. Rehearse. It's the single most important step you can take to become a better speaker. If you rehearse, you'll be able to give the speech to the audience. If you don't, you'll still be getting to know it yourself. The difference is enormous in terms of what the audience can get out of your presentation.

Second, let's agree that you won't rehearse in front of a mirror alone. That trick fails to mimic adequately what public speaking is actually like. But more than that, it actually can create a problem for some: greater self-consciousness.

Self-forgetfulness is the secret to great speech making.

Successful public speaking comes ultimately from focusing less on yourself and more on the audience. For now, take it as the big Zen insight of this book. *If you can forget about yourself—and even your speech—in the moment of giving it and instead focus on what the audience is getting from you, your presentations will be transformed into joyous performances.*

The point of rehearsal is to take the first steps toward that optimal state by working through all the self-conscious moments and potentially awkward transitions that otherwise will trip you up during the presentation itself.

Rehearsal, in the first instance, is where you find out what your story is, as you put the whole thing together for the first time orally. It's not enough to do it in your head. Only in speaking aloud will you discover where the gaps are, the pieces that you thought connected but in fact do not.

Stage actors typically rehearse for up to six weeks before they begin to perform. They leave absolutely nothing to chance. And yet a CEO of a Fortune 500 company will stand up in front of his stockholders with literally billions at stake (not to mention his job) and "wing it."

And you will too, despite having read these words. So let me urge you once again: Rehearse, even for those "little" presentations. You can either change the world a little bit at a time, or you can leave no trace that you were ever here.

The speaker's focus should be on the audience; the audience's should be on the content.

Let's be optimistic and imagine that you have rehearsed your content, and you've found the kinesthetic moments that will allow you to connect powerfully with your audience during the performance itself. And now, suddenly, it's time to present.

My fifth-grade math teacher loved multicolored chalk. He'd stand in front of us, holding the chalk in his hands, more or less at parade rest at his sides. As he stood there, a multicolored sheen would develop on the sides of his trousers.

Naturally, we, his students, made fun of this addition to his garments. But the real fun began when we asked him questions and he thought about the answers. Then, his hands would creep up to his face. It's a common gesture connected with thinking or other kinds of preoccupation—you bring your hands to your chin, your cheeks, your hair. Anywhere around your face.

Thus, the multicolored sheen would begin to develop on his face. Well, that was pretty great. But if we asked him a question that really gave him pause, gradually, his hand would steal over to his nose, and he would stick the piece of chalk right up it.

We loved it! Our whole aim in math class became asking questions that would cause the teacher to stick chalk up his nose. Unfortunately, I didn't learn much fifth-grade math as a result. But I did learn something very telling about public speaking.

Visual distractions (indeed, any kind of distraction) can easily prevent an audience from getting even the little they can get under optimal conditions from a speech.

Or to put it another, more positive, way: As you speak, you send out a host of nonverbal communications with your face, your body, your posture, your gestures, the tone of your voice, and above all the way you move in relation to your audience. If those communications are consistent with and support your primary message—the content of your presentation—you can give a powerful speech. If, on the other hand, there is an inconsistency, or a competing message, the nonverbal one will win every time.

Every one of us can recall a teacher or speaker we've watched whose intellectual message was lost because the hapless performer's fly was unzipped, or he paced back and forth in oblivion until we thought we would go mad, or, more subtly, the presenter's monotonous voice merged with the white noise from the slide projector until all we could hear was an undifferentiated roar. The next thing we know, we're snapping back to alertness and realizing we haven't been truly present in the room for some uncertain length of time and we've lost the thread of the talk.

The goal in performance, then, is to support the core message you've crafted with voice and expression and gesture and motion so that both verbal and nonverbal unite in a powerful expression of your ideas. That is what making a kinesthetic connection is all about.

Great public speakers listen to their audiences.

In reality, your job as a public speaker is to listen. Does that sound odd? How can I listen, you say, when I have to do most of the talking? But the opportunities for listening abound throughout a presentation. Remember the two CEOs I described in the introduction? Which one do you most closely resemble? When you first begin to speak, saying something along the lines of "hello," do you wait for a response, or do you plunge on regardless of what the audience says back to you? If you wait, and genuinely look for some kind of response from the audience, even in that little moment, you will begin to create a real bond with the audience. The people in front of you will say to themselves, "Oh, she really cares about this audience or this talk." If, on the other hand, you utter your opening phrases and instantly launch into your talk, the message the audience receives is, "This person is too nervous to connect with me, or too indifferent, or too programmed. He just wants to get done."

A successful connection with the audience comes from countless little moments like this. You don't have to be a Patrick Henry or a Daniel Webster or a Ronald Reagan to become a charismatic speaker. You do have to connect with the audience. And you do have to express your passion to them. Oddly enough, openness to the audience fosters both impressions.

Think about it from the audience's point of view. You're the expert. The audience has granted you the power, for now, of informing and persuading it, and that audience is very curious about what kind of experience the next hour is going to be. An audience expects you to be a little nervous at first—everyone in that audience has some idea about just how hard it is to do what you're doing. Imagine if you seem genuinely interested right from the start in whether or not the listeners are getting the message. You must really care; this speech must be important to you. That's the real beginning of charisma: caring. The word itself comes from the Greek (naturally), meaning favor or grace, as in someone divinely infused with passion. And how do we detect passion? When it can't stay contained within one individual. When it overflows and threatens to engulf us, too. When it causes someone to grab us and not let go.

That person cares, we think. That person has passion. That person is charismatic. And unless those impressions are undercut by nonverbal communications during the course of a presentation, they will be what people take away from the event.

Ultimately, great public speaking comes from passion.

Later on, we'll talk about some technical details of voice, face, gesture, posture, and motion during delivery. We'll talk about the notorious Mehrabian study that many speech coaches use incorrectly to suggest that "93 percent of communication is visual." Thus, they argue, the content hardly matters. It's all about looking good. Nothing could be further from the truth. The Mehrabian study *assumed* that content was the most important element of communication. But we'll look at the range of modern communications research for what it can tell us about how to communicate consistently and powerfully, with your verbal and nonverbal messages coherent and strong. We'll also look at what the Greeks had to say about delivery and audience—how to think about them, woo them, trick them, move them. And how to avoid being wooed, tricked, or moved—about which the Greeks, as cynical and practical as we are today, also had much to say.

In addition, we'll learn how to "read" an audience so that you can listen and watch the people in front of you as you're presenting, to ensure you and your audience both become and stay powerfully connected. We'll study the five continua of audience connection I've developed for use in special situations such as sales presentations, as well as generally for persuasive speeches. And we'll look at Q&A sessions and other kinds of audience involvement in some detail.

The key to remember is that all of the technical details are only worth paying attention to if they allow you to focus better on the audience and to eliminate the contradictions that too many speakers portray between verbal and nonverbal communications. To enable you, in short, to give an audience-centered speech.

All too often the focus is somewhere else, and the result is boring. The presenter's content speaks of how vital this marketing plan is to the future of the company, for example, but the voice is a monotone, so that the stronger, nonverbal message is, "I say this is important but I don't really mean it. I'm bored with it, too. If I really cared, my voice would be rising in excitement as I talked about it."

Or again, the content says this is the essence of how we're going to turn this company around and become profitable again, but the speaker is backing away as she says it, visibly signaling a lack of real commitment to the turnaround.

I once saw a consultant give a speech to a meeting of a client's board. He had some hard truths to present about the ability of the company to cope with the conflict and the difficulty that lay ahead. His message, essentially, was that the company was not facing up to its situation, but that the consultant and his team would help the client really wrestle, for the first time, with the core issues. As he said this, he moved backward until he was leaning comfortably against the wall of the conference room! The nonverbal message, that the consultant wasn't really keen to grapple with the tough issues, was the one that the board retained. It quickly moved to terminate the contract and hire someone else.

Great public speakers communicate enthusiasm at some level to their audiences. Even if the topic is serious, underneath that emotion lies a real enthusiasm in having the chance to talk about it. To put it simply, if you're having a good time, the audience will, too.

To get to that point, we have a lot of work to do. You will need to develop great audience-centered content. You will need to rehearse that content. And you will need to learn how to rise above self-absorption to deliver a speech that is truly "given" to the audience. But the good news is that it begins with you and your passion for the subject you want to talk about it. If you have that, all the rest will follow. You can be compelling, you can achieve a powerful connection with your audience, you can be memorable. You can even be charismatic, by being most resolutely and honestly yourself. Successful public speaking is not, in the end, trickery or technique. It is passion.

Remember

- Public speaking is structured conversation.

- Audiences come into a presentation asking, "Why am I here?"

- If you're successful, they will leave asking, "How do I implement these ideas?"

- Focus your speech on one key message.

- Connect with your audience by telling them stories.

- Give your speech to the members of the audience by allowing them to become active.

- The single most important thing you can do to prepare a speech is to rehearse.

- The speaker's focus should be on the audience; the audience's should be on the content.

- Great public speakers listen to their audiences.

- Ultimately, great public speaking comes from passion.

PART II

Preparing the Content

CHAPTER 3

Understand the Audience

A STANDARD MODEL OF COMMUNICATION has the following parts: sender, medium, message, receiver, feedback, and noise. During a presentation, the first five elements have to be performing optimally, and the last minimally, in order for communication to take place. And yet, if you think about how most people approach the onerous chore of presenting, it often appears that they only consider the first two elements, perhaps the first three. They obsess about themselves and the technology. They worry about the content. But the receiver—the audience—gets scant attention, except perhaps as a faceless, scary mass. Feedback is a subject usually avoided altogether, or thought about briefly with true terror ("What if they ask me a question I can't answer?"). Noise, the sixth element, is the result, usually compounded by a lack of rehearsal.

Great speakers listen to their audiences.

The successful presenter reverses this unfortunate polarity and instead focuses on receiver, feedback, and noise suppression. You can only do this if you're well prepared. You can only be forgetful of the sender and the medium if you've got the message down cold and you know exactly how you're going to put it over.

In this context, think of a speech not as a presentation but as an opportunity to *listen to your audience*. I will keep returning to that dictum as we work through the process I have developed for creating powerful content.

Here's the process as a quick list:

- Understand the audience.

- Craft the elevator speech.

- Pick the level of need.

- Find the story.

- Structure the content.

- Make the journey.

- Involve the audience.

In order to be a successful public speaker, one who connects with audiences powerfully, makes an impact on them, and moves them to action, you have to shift your orientation. You need to think of yourself as a strong listener who carefully guides the audience where you want it to go, rather than as an orator who declaims like a professor, or a politician on the stump, or a lawyer summing up before a jury. *You need listen to your audience.*

What does this bold statement actually mean?

You are there because of them. A presentation doesn't happen unless the audience gets it. Literally. Let me say that again another way: Your speech has mattered only if the audience has heard it. So you won't actually know if your speech making has been a waste of time or not unless you do listen to your audience.

How does this work in practice? You have to let go of your own adrenaline-filled self-consciousness and begin to look at your audience. How are they doing? Are they attentive? Are they looking at you or out the window? Are they rapt, still, comfortable, or are they shifting in their chairs? Do they respond to your wit, your jokes, or are they inert? Are they leaning actively forward in their chairs, or sitting passively back, telegraphing inertia? In short, what is their emotional and intellectual state? You need to know this in order to know how to shape your presentation for best effect.

Think about the goal we have set ourselves to reach for in giving a speech. *The only reason to give a speech is to change the world.* In the case of the politician and the lawyer, the object is to move the audience to action of some kind—votes, a conviction, or an acquittal—but we're after something even more basic, something stronger, something ultimately more important.

Aristotle was wrong: All speeches are persuasive acts.

We want to persuade people to do something new. That's a tall order. But that is the essence of speech making: to move people to action. Anything else is wasted effort, because people simply don't remember much of what they hear. It's not a good format for imparting information. It is a good format for persuading people to believe in or act on something. (And just to drive a stake through the heart of one evil demon: Contrary to popular belief, PowerPoint slides don't increase retention rates much, if at all. Indeed, most PowerPoint presentations are in fact speech outlines put together for the speaker's benefit, not the audience's. The result is a distraction that actually drives comprehension down, as the audience tries to match the words on the screen with what is coming out of the speaker's mouth. You're giving the audience twice as much to do and two places to look. Bad idea.)

Aristotle got it wrong. He said there were three kinds of speeches: informative, persuasive, and "decorative"—speeches of praise and the like. But there really is only one kind: the persuasive. When the secretary of defense gives a briefing to the press on the war effort, is that an informative speech? Not really. What's actually going on is that the secretary of defense is persuading the press that he's in control, in command of the situation, and that the war is going well. To be sure, some facts, some bits of information, are conveyed from speaker to audience. But the primary purpose is a different kind of show. And the extent to which the secretary is aware of his real purpose, and can focus on that, is the extent to which he will be successful. If he thinks that his purpose is exchanging information, then he's in a game of "gotcha" with the press. He gives out information, and the press tries to prove him wrong.

If instead he's being a persuasive leader, then he doesn't have to know all the details. He can turn the briefing over to someone else for areas of expertise he doesn't possess. All he has to do is act like the man in charge.

A classic instance of this point is the games played during the 2000 campaign and President Bush's early weeks in office, when the press tried to catch him out on the names of foreign leaders and the like. Because Bush allowed the issue to become one of his expertise rather than his leadership abilities, what he knew and didn't know became fair game. And the results were predictably disastrous.

So how can we take a page from the politician's book of painful learning and ensure that the topic of a presentation gets framed the way it should, that the issue is one of persuasion, not information, and that you as speaker are allowed to shine—and to change the world?

Note that an important shift takes place as soon as you realize that you're seeking to persuade, not inform. *In all cases.* The focus has to shift to the audience, because "persuade" is a verb that calls for an object: Persuade whom? Information can be given out, but not received. But persuasion requires a party of the second part.

This insight works just as well for presentations to five or fifty people at internal meetings as it does for the president of the United States. As soon as you set yourself up as someone who has all the answers, you invite people to raise objections. If instead you seek to enlist your audience to work with you to achieve a goal, one that involves action on the audience's part, then you invite people to help you make your ideas work. It's a subtle shift, but an enormously powerful one.

So we listen to the audience, from start to finish, in real time, as the presentation happens. And to make that possible, we have to begin by shaping the content of the speech in terms of the audience's needs. The first step in this process of creating audience-centered content is to figure out who's in the audience, and what their needs and expectations are. Second, we'll focus the content once and for all by deciding upon what we call the *elevator speech*—in some ways the most difficult step in preparing a speech, since it involves thinking hard about what you are not going to say. Third, we'll look at the level of need you'll be addressing. This step is important because it determines, in essence, how hard your "sell" will be. It stands to reason that if you're making a speech about a fire in a crowded theater, you'll get the audience's attention. Someone else trying to sell Milk Duds will go unheeded.

Fourth, you'll decide overall what kind of story will help you get your message across to the audience. There are a few basic stories that have nearly universal resonance, and picking one of those will ensure that your audience can quickly and as effortlessly as possible orient themselves to your message in a way that makes them receptive. It's a way of framing the presentation that puts it in a context that connects with an audience at a deep, intuitive level.

Fifth, you'll structure the arguments and information you will actually present in ways that are as time-honored as the ancient

Greeks' understanding of speech structure, and as modern as recent psychological insights into the way the brain works and what motivates people to action.

Finally, as part of that structure, you'll figure out ways to involve the audience kinesthetically, visually, and aurally.

Now, let's get down to the details.

Determine everything you can about the audience.

First, you need to spend some time thinking hard about the audience itself in very basic ways. Who are they? What do they fear? What do they want? Spend some real time developing detailed answers to these key questions. Note that the first questions we ask involve emotions—fears and wants. If you don't understand those key motivators, then you'll never be able to connect with the people in the audience. As I will say more than once, great presentations are both emotional and intellectual journeys that you, the speaker, and the audience take together. You can't take an audience on that journey unless you know what its hopes, fears, and motivations are.

How do you get that information? If you don't know already, if you're presenting to a group of people who are relatively unknown to you, begin with the person or group that talked you into giving the presentation. Then research the group or the audience in all the ways you can imagine—the Internet, periodicals, books, whatever seems likely to be useful.

Then gather the rest of the information:

- What is the age range of the audience?

- What is its socioeconomic makeup?

- Are you speaking in your first language? Theirs?

- How different are you from them?

- What do you have in common?

- What is their status compared to yours—higher, lower, the same?

- Have they had any bad news recently? Any good news?

- Do you know anyone in the audience? Would it be appropriate to address them directly?

Each of these questions has implications for how you will shape your comments. You want to match your talk to the age range of the audience without talking down to the young. You need to give thought to what you may have in common with a group that comes from a very different socioeconomic group than your own. Everyone has fears and dreams. Start there.

If you're speaking to a group for whom your language is non-native, then eliminate as many of your colloquialisms as possible, and slow down a little. It's the colloquialisms and jokes that give foreign speakers the most trouble.

The most important act of imagination, however, is to figure out what the audience's emotional state is. If you know what they wish for, and what they are afraid of, you can talk to any audience with a chance at making a real connection.

Get with the program.

Once you've figured out the emotional state of the people in front of you, ask questions about the event:

- When is the speech to be given?

- Who comes before you?

- Who comes after?

- What kind of an occasion is it?

- How many people will be in the room?

- What are they expecting?

- Are you the after-dinner entertainment, or a keynoter?

If you're speaking after dinner, plan to speak for about twelve minutes at the most. If you're the keynote speaker, you can go longer. I like hour-long time slots with time left for interaction, say, forty-five minutes of planned talk, interrupted occasionally with about fifteen minutes of unscripted interaction. Some events and conferences plan segments that go as long as ninety minutes. I find that, in most cases, what can be said in ninety minutes can be said more succinctly in sixty with a little more preparation and thought. I have rarely witnessed a ninety-minute talk that truly had a half-hour of extra meat in it. No one ever wishes a speech would run longer, or is sorry if one ends early.

And while I'm on the subject, if the typical attention span is something like twenty minutes, then in an hour's presentation, there should be at least three opportunities for questions—after twenty minutes, forty minutes, and near the end. Breaks like that not only allow audiences to catch up and clarify anything they may have missed, but the pauses also allow audiences to recharge and refresh.

All of these questions, and any others you can think of, will help you develop a sense of who the audience is that you'll be addressing. The more you know about the people in front of you, the better you'll know how to connect with them. One of the best ways to warm up the connection with an audience, for example, is to personalize your presentation so that you refer to specific members of the audience and specific events that are important to them, not to mention cultural touchstones and inside references. Of course, all this can be carried too far, and must be done with tact. But more speeches err on the side of impersonality than on the excessively cozy and intimate. Connecting with your audience begins with knowing as much about them and the occasion as possible.

Make an effort, too, to think consciously about how you and the audience are *alike*. What hopes, fears, dreams do you share? Are you similar in outlook, age, experience? One of the simple ways to connect with an audience is to bridge the gaps between you and it by finding ways in which you are similar. The results can be extraordinary. Former First Lady Barbara Bush connected powerfully with some inner-city children during one of her literacy tours by sitting down with them and openly discussing her own childhood dreams and fears. Soon they were opening up and telling her about theirs. She had managed to find the universal connection between a privileged woman of power and rank and a group of poor elementary schoolkids. With a little work and imagination, it can be done.

Remember

- A standard model of communication has the following parts: sender, medium, message, receiver, feedback, and noise.

- Each is important to successful public speaking.

- Think of a presentation as an opportunity to listen to your audience.

- Find out everything you possibly can about your audience and plan to communicate with that unique group, no other.

CHAPTER 4

Craft the Elevator Speech

O NCE WE KNOW THE AUDIENCE AS intimately as we can, then it's time to begin to focus the content in terms of the audience. We begin with the elevator speech. Recall that audiences only remember something like 10 percent to 30 percent of what they hear. If we think of a speech as a very limited act of persuasion, then it follows that we need to be very clear what we're trying to persuade the audience of. The elevator speech will help us do that. It is, simply, a one-sentence expression of the main reason that you're giving the speech—on the audience's terms.

Here's the scenario: You're the keynote speaker at a conference. You're up early on the day of the speech, a little nervous (perhaps more than a little), and a little early getting down to the mezzanine floor of the hotel where the ballroom and your appointment with destiny are. You get on the elevator at the fourteenth floor and hit the button for mezzanine. As the elevator heads down, it stops on the twelfth floor, and a cheery-looking convention delegate with a similar name tag gets on. He determines that the elevator's heading to the floor he wants, and faces forward.

His eyes shift over to you and your name tag. There's an immediate (and gratifying) look of recognition in his eyes. "Oh," he says, "You're the keynote."

"Yes," you admit.

"I'm a golfer, and there is a PGA-class golf course outside. So tell me, why should I attend your speech?" he asks, being a little bit of a smart aleck, and showing that he's someone who's attended enough keynotes to know that this crucial detail is worth checking out.

What you say then is the elevator speech. One sentence (you don't have time for any more) that will motivate this person to attend your speech rather than head out early to the golf course.

What do you say?

You say something like, "Because if you attend my speech, you will learn how to give presentations without fear, presentations that move your audience to action every time."

My guess is that your interlocutor will attend the event.

What are the elements of the elevator speech? First of all, it must contain *a benefit for the potential member of the audience.* Something that the person in question will get out of attending. In this case, it's learning how to give speeches without fear, speeches that move your audience.

Second, it must contain the word *you,* meaning the audience. That's to make sure that you keep your attention directly focused where it belongs, on the audience.

Third, it must contain some reference to emotion. In this case, it's the fear that is usually connected with public speaking. Why? Because emotion is more engaging, and more memorable, than intellectual information. Emotion polarizes people. They are much more likely to react than not. A small number of people may respond by saying, "I don't need that; I'm never afraid of public speaking." But that's a very small number indeed; you won't lose many potential members of the audience that way. And you'll gain a whole lot more who do connect with the word and the emotion.

Gear your elevator speech toward solving your audience's problems.

Most Americans have at least heard of President John F. Kennedy's inaugural address, the one in which he urged his fellow citizens to "ask not what your country can do for you—ask what you can do for your country." The elevator speech for that address might be something like the following:

Together, you and I can fight Soviet aggression with a strong defense and a strong economy and by helping the rest of the free world.

What's the benefit to the audience? It gets to go on living; at the time, there was real fear of the Soviet threat that included nuclear aggression. The emotion is fear—and patriotism. Note how the emotional message could have polarized Americans. Perhaps not everyone thought that the Soviet threat was real or was worried about communists taking over the world. But Kennedy gave people a positive side to the message as well. Just about everyone wants a strong economy, after all.

It's difficult to keep political addresses focused because of the temptation at moments like this to offer a little something to everyone. But Kennedy's address was better focused than most, and the elevator speech shows how he and his team managed it.

Once you've figured out what your elevator speech is, then use that to guide all the rest of the content development. Everything that doesn't relate to the elevator speech, no matter how fascinating or exciting to you, must be eliminated. If information doesn't support the key concept, it doesn't belong in your speech.

Far more speeches fail from a surfeit of information than a deficit. Far too many businesspeople think of a presentation as a data dump—the opportunity to show the audience what they know about a subject.

But that's not interesting to audiences. What they do care about is how some of the information that you have can help them solve their problems. The elevator speech helps you keep focused on that crucial insight, and it helps keep you focused on the audience itself.

It's worth repeating: You must focus on one idea and one idea only. Give your audience more than that, and it will quickly get lost in your information, trying desperately to remember irrelevant details and feeling betrayed by you. The audience will think that you've led them astray. Many speakers overprepare, because they are afraid that they'll get asked something they don't know. But what audiences want is not to be buried in detail, but for you to tell them what's important, what the key concepts are, what the essence of a body of knowledge is.

Armed with only the material that supports your one key idea, you're ready to develop the structure of your presentation.

Remember

- Focus your talk on one idea, the essential idea for your audience.

- Summarize that idea in an elevator speech of one sentence.

- The sentence should contain a benefit for the audience, the word *you*, and a reference to emotion.

- Use the elevator speech to focus the rest of your content development.

CHAPTER 5

Pick the Level of Need

YOU NEED TO DECIDE WHERE TO locate the topic of your presentation on the relative scale of needs we all possess. How important is your speech to its audience? This exercise will help you further shape the content by determining the kinds of examples you use, the claims you make, and the stories you tell.

In the 1960s, humanistic psychologist Abraham Maslow developed a hierarchy of needs that has stood the test of time very well. Maslow described a pyramid with physiological needs at the bottom, followed by safety, social needs like love and belonging, ego needs like esteem, and self-actualization.

His basic point was that we satisfy those needs in order from lowest to highest. In other words, if we're lacking food or shelter, we can't be concerned with anything higher up on the pyramid, like love, for instance. As we satisfy needs lower on the list, we turn to the next one up. Once we've worked our way to the top of the pyramid, we begin to worry about realizing our inner selves, or getting our golf handicap down to a respectable level.

Now turn that pyramid on its head and think about how deeply a presentation can engage you. If the issue is the safety of your business (The Japanese are eating your lunch! The start-ups are going to steal your customers and render your business model obsolete!) then you're going to pay better attention than if the issue is simply how respected you are in the industry. Respect is nice, but survival comes first.

Decide how important your presentation is to the audience.

The idea is that you need to decide at what level on the pyramid of needs you're going to aim your speech. Here, the lower on the pyramid you go (ideally to the safety level) the more viscerally and powerfully you're going to engage your audience. But it has to be real, and it has to be consistent. Don't begin a pitch by claiming that the audience is in imminent peril if it doesn't listen and then proceed to talk about the importance of treating your people right, unless you're prepared to back up your claims with good data that shows that companies that ignore their people suffer declining profit margins and eventually go out of business.

Take a relatively recent, high-profile example. Recall the Clinton–Bush election of 1992 in which Clinton dashed around the country "feeling our pain." That was essentially a love message. Bush had great trouble articulating a reason why he should be president. Frequently he talked about our international stature—an esteem issue. Neither man engaged the voters much until Clinton realized that "It's the economy, stupid," and he started talking about how too many people were left out of the prosperity that America held out as a cornerstone of the American dream.

That's a safety issue. In this way, Clinton pulled the electorate down to the level where people begin to pay attention, and he began to move in the polls.

In the Bush–Gore election of 2000, neither candidate came up with a clear overall message. Pollsters had indicated that education was an important issue, but neither candidate could frame the issue in a way that located it clearly on the lower end of the hierarchy of needs. As a result, while we all believe that in some sense education is important, we tuned out of the election process en masse. Bush tried the old Republican issue of defense and our national military readiness, which gets a response in some quarters, among people who really do feel threatened by China or Russia, but before September 11 the issue was too abstract to grab most voters. Since the economy was still perceived to be in pretty good shape, the personal pocketbook safety issue wasn't available. The result was a lack of engagement. Pundits blamed the alienation of the populace on a lot of things, including the populace itself, but no one put the issue squarely where it belonged: The candidates didn't have a clear message that dealt with their audience's needs in a visceral way.

How can you expect people to listen avidly to what you have to say if you don't make an effort to address them in their terms? Why should they care?

I worked recently with a consultant who regularly presented on the issue of cyberterrorists bringing down the Web sites of large corporations. Surprisingly, as presented, this issue didn't seem to grab the attention of the audiences of Fortune 500 companies for whom it was intended. As we worked on the speech, we realized that, in an effort to be intellectual and dispassionate, the consultant had focused on the financial cost of hacking. While significant, the numbers themselves weren't conveying much meaning. Millions of abstract dollars simply don't make the leaders of large multinationals hold their breath. I coached the consultant to weave in a few stories of the embarrassment and loss of corporate integrity caused by some recent hacking incidents. We recast the speech in terms of the potential threat to the safety of the companies through their Web sites, and the interest level of the audiences shot right up.

So translate the hierarchy of needs into business terms and see where your topic stacks up. There's nothing wrong with talking about community issues, or the respect of the industry, or even how to drive your company to become the best company it can be, but understand that anyone who talks the corporate equivalent of safety (the life and death of the business) will grab and hold the attention of an audience. Everyone else's efforts will pale by comparison.

Remember

- Place the main thrust of your speech on the hierarchy of psychological needs.

- The further down the hierarchy you position your speech, the more viscerally you will grab your audience's attention.

- Safety is a prime issue with which to engage your audience, but don't claim a safety issue if you can't support it.

Kennedy at the Berlin Wall

H as one of your speeches ever caused your listeners to riot in the streets for three days? That was the result of President John F. Kennedy's June 26, 1963, address to the citizens of Berlin. More than a million of them lined the Rudolf Wilde Platz in the divided city to hear the young American president who had been so severely tested on his resistance to communism by the Bay of Pigs fiasco, the Cuban Missile Crisis, and the Berlin Wall itself. It may well have been the largest gathering of its kind in human history.

Within a few minutes, speaking through an interpreter, Kennedy created a delirium of enthusiasm in his listeners, causing them to demonstrate for three days until the police and military were able to bring control once again to the streets.

What was the secret of Kennedy's power? How did he connect so strongly with his audience? What are the lessons of this short, simple, and yet extraordinary speech? Can they be applied to the more ordinary venues and situations that face other presenters?

Understand what the audience needs.

First of all, consider how Maslow's hierarchy of needs applies to this case. The citizens of Berlin were threatened. They felt cut off from the Western world. Their safety was at stake. And Kennedy addressed that issue by making common cause with them—"*Ich bin ein Berliner*."

The rhetoric was powerful, even though it apparently meant "I am a jelly doughnut." (A Berliner is a favorite German pastry much like a jelly doughnut. The correct way to say it would have been "*Ich bin Berliner*.")

Look at the end of the short speech. The Berliners were wondering, would Americans stand by them? Kennedy brilliantly and elegantly addressed that concern by talking about freedom being indivisible.

> *So let me ask you, as I close, to lift your eyes beyond the dangers of today, to the hopes of tomorrow, beyond the freedom merely of this city of Berlin, or your country of Germany, to the advance of freedom everywhere, beyond the wall to the day of peace with justice, beyond yourselves and ourselves to all mankind.*
>
> *Freedom is indivisible, and when one man is enslaved, all are not free. When all are free, then we can look forward to that day when this city will be joined as one and this country and this great continent of Europe in a peaceful and hopeful globe. When that day finally comes, as it will, the people of West Berlin can take sober satisfaction in the fact that they were in the front lines for almost two decades.*
>
> *All free men, wherever they may live, are citizens of Berlin, and, therefore, as a free man, I take pride in the words Ich bin ein Berliner.*

By making common cause with them around the issue of freedom, Kennedy met the most deep-seated fears of the audience with reassurance. "*Ich bin ein Berliner*" was exactly what the city wanted to hear.

Identify with your audience—early in the speech.

Second, Kennedy made the speech audience-centered. He identified with the audience, using the German phrase about doughnuts, early in the speech.

You can't preach to an audience about grand things if the audience perceives you to be standing aloof to them. It's another paradox that gives speakers trouble. You need to find the ways in which you and the audience are alike, and make those clear early on. In that way, your listeners will be willing to open themselves to your message. It's a way of building trust quickly. Audiences want their speakers to have credibility, and they want to be able to trust them. You can't create the latter unless you find a way to connect with your audience.

Kennedy accomplishes his identification with the Berliners with the famous phrase, which he utters in the first minute of his speech: "Two thousand years ago the proudest boast was *Civis Romanus sum*. Today, in the world of freedom, the proudest boast is *Ich bin ein Berliner*." Of course, the President goes on to cement the identification with his brief sermon on freedom, but the initial move comes early, before the important themes of the talk have been established. Thus, Kennedy realizes that the first step he has to take is one toward his audience, in the essential figurative sense that shows that he understands their problems.

Beyond Maslow's hierarchy, we can discover a few other lessons of great speech making. First, write it yourself. Don't let the communications department do it. It won't sound like you. It won't be personal. Second, keep it simple and true. Never speak down to your audience, but never try to impress them just for the sake of impressing them. Third, appeal to something larger than self-interest. That's essential where public rhetoric is concerned. Finally, repeat a memorable phrase often. Repetition, especially in front of huge audiences that take time to get your message, is key. But note that Kennedy doesn't repeat the concepts—that's boring—just the memorable phrase.

Write it yourself.

Kennedy wrote the short speech himself and insisted on delivering it over the objections of the military command, who worried that the speech would cause the nervous citizens of Berlin to riot, as they in fact did. But the point is that Kennedy avoided the bureaucratic and lengthy in his talk at least in part because he didn't have the time to create anything wordier. He wrote the speech in haste over the few days prior to the event, on his way to Berlin. Lacking the usual governmental resources to help him, he was forced to keep it simple.

The speech also reflected his beliefs more closely than a speech penned by his speechwriters could have. And that's the first lesson for business speakers. Rather than having your staff prepare some notes for what they think you should say, take the time to figure out the main points for yourself. Then get your researchers to fill in any missing detail. That way the presentation is more likely to reflect your beliefs and thinking.

Keep it simple and true.

This speech belongs to a select group of memorable speeches that clock in at roughly ten minutes or less and stick to one clear theme. It is the coincidence of brevity, simplicity, and integrity with an important occasion that makes for golden rhetoric. Many presentations are long-winded and simple-minded, but few manage to say the right thing at the right time in the fewest possible words. Lincoln's Gettysburg Address, Martin Luther King, Jr.'s "I Have a Dream" speech, and even the Sermon on the Mount combine these ingredients unforgettably. Reagan's elegy on the subject of the Challenger disaster comes close; time will be the judge of that speech's staying power. In each case, the absolute clarity and conviction of the speaker about what needed to be said on an important occasion came first. Then came the simplicity of delivery. Finally, the success of the speech in the moment ensured that history would remember it forever.

In Kennedy's case, the speech is about freedom, and the unity of all free peoples, including the citizens of Berlin. The enemy of freedom is communism, says Kennedy, but it cannot prevail against free peoples everywhere. That's it. "Freedom has many difficulties, and democracy is not perfect, but we have never had to put up a wall to keep our people in," says Kennedy, and the words are unforgettable because he confronts directly and without flinching the hard reality facing Berliners. He meets the seriousness of the political crisis with matching passion and strength.

Appeal to something larger than self-interest.

We humans are at once noble and selfish. If you appeal solely to our self-interest, we will listen, and perhaps appreciate your words. But we won't respect you. We know what pandering is and are quick to recognize it. The tendency to pander is what makes most political speeches today so forgettable. Kennedy understood that a principle was at stake, one that might be difficult and dangerous to uphold for the citizens of Berlin (and the free world) but one that was worth the fight. To really get your audience on its feet—and rioting—you have to show them how self-interest and larger principles coincide, such that personal sacrifice is worth it if it becomes necessary.

Repeat a memorable phrase or two often.

Even in this short speech there is a good deal of repetition. It is the single most important linguistic device of speech making. Audiences have difficulty remembering what they hear—all the studies show that listeners retain only a small percentage of the presentations they witness—and repetition helps them keep up and gives them a sense of mastery of the occasion. So resist the temptation to try to be clever at your audience's expense. Instead, look for ways to repeat your basic theme memorably. Kennedy uses the *"Ich bin ein Berliner"* line twice, at the beginning and the end of the speech, but he repeats another key phrase as well.

> *There are many people in the world who really don't understand, or say they don't, what is the great issue between the free world and the communist world. Let them come to Berlin. There are some who say that communism is the wave of the future. Let them come to Berlin. And there are some who say in Europe and elsewhere we can work with the communists. Let them come to Berlin. And there are even a few who say that it is true that communism is an evil system, but it permits us to make economic progress.* Lass' sie nach Berlin kommen. *Let them come to Berlin.*

Good book title

It's rare that the historical moment, the cause, and the speaker come together to produce unforgettable speech making, but when it does the words can echo down the years to inspire us when the moment, the cause, and the speaker are gone. And we can take the lessons of the historical moment and apply them to our own. Great rhetoric may be the result. Even if your listeners don't finally riot in the streets.

CHAPTER 6

Find the Story

S O YOU'VE FOCUSED ON YOUR AUDIENCE
by learning as much about them as you can.
You've developed a one-sentence summary
—the elevator speech—of your intended talk in terms of what it
might mean to this audience. And you've positioned your talk on
the audience's hierarchy of needs, so you know how important it
is to them.

It's time to begin to shape the content itself. And to do that
effectively, you need to decide what story you're telling.

A great deal has been written about the importance of storytelling, and most presenters today have some sense that they should
tell stories during the course of their speeches. But that's usually
as far as it goes. As a result, speeches are filled with anecdotes,
some relevant, some not, and the speech can disintegrate into a

loose collection of bits and pieces, any one of which might make sense, but which together don't necessarily make a cohesive whole.

Worse, many a speech now begins and ends with supposedly charming personal anecdotes of limited relevance and less point from businesspeople whose lives lack the excitement necessary for good storytelling.

There is a better way.

Connect to an archetypal story structure.

Fortunately for public speakers (and audiences) everywhere, human culture is based on stories—call them collective myths or archetypes—that shape how we experience and understand the world. It's these stories you need to invoke to bring your presentations up to the level of great speech making.

Because we're imbued with these stories from an early age, we don't feel like our lives have meaning unless we can connect in some way to one of them. Why more businesses and organizations don't understand this important need for meaning is puzzling. The organizations that do provide a myth-making element for the workplace inspire great loyalty and hard work in their employees.

The psychologist Carl G. Jung first articulated this approach to understanding human psychology and motivation, although of course his work was based on Freud and others, as well as the ethnographers who first began to collect folk tales and other mythic stories more than a century before.

But perhaps the most powerful expression of our collective mythic meaning-making is to be found in Joseph Campbell's work, particularly *The Hero with a Thousand Faces*.

In this book, Campbell described a hero's journey, a basic quest, as a powerful, ancient means we humans have of creating social meaning and of understanding our life roles. Why are we here? What are we supposed to do with our lives? What makes one life meaningful and another empty?

It's in an effort to answer questions like these, Campbell and the others suggest, that humans have created the myths of each culture. Hollywood has taken up Campbell's ideas with enthusiasm, and many writers and directors have quite consciously used them to create some of the world's most successful movies, such as the *Star Wars* trilogy, the Indiana Jones movies, and a host of others.

Some years ago, it occurred to me that one of the reasons why modern public speaking (especially business presentations) lacked punch and interest was that it rarely told good strong stories. Campbell's work illuminated a way to improve on that sorry record. My own work as a political speechwriter had convinced me more than fifteen years ago that we needed to go beyond simply telling anecdotes to draw upon deep mythic *Story*. Politicians have known for a long time, at least since Lincoln, and relearned from Reagan, the importance of telling stories. But few have made the leap from stories to Story. The ones that do usually get reelected and revered as spokespeople for a time or a generation. When FDR talked the United States out of the Depression, for example, he told a story of hope that resonated with a people desperate for precisely that. He made the leap.

Even today, when many presenters and speech coaches pay lip service to the importance of telling stories, few understand the difference or are willing to do the hard work to create Story. We are all storytellers now, but all too often that only means an anecdote.

What's the difference? It lies precisely in these deep, cultural Stories like the Hero's Journey or Quest. Speeches today are rife with stories, but few are structured properly to draw upon the strength of Story. This work is not easy to do; it involves thinking hard about what you're trying to say and to whom you are trying to say it. Presentations that draw upon these mythic structures have a power and resonance unlike others, and they represent audience-centered speaking at its most profound.

In my work as a speech coach over the years, I have also become aware that the Quest story is not the only one that has power for business audiences. We need to add a few others to complete the list and give presenters a full range of choices from which to craft the best possible speech. Invoking one of these basic stories instantly orients your audience, because it will know deeply and intuitively what mental model you are putting forward. Moreover, these basic stories put your audience in particular frames of mind and emotional states, and lead them to particular expected outcomes. If you weave these stories properly into your presentations, you will find that audiences respond enthusiastically to your point of view and to the actions you wish them to take.

Finding the Story

What are these basic stories? Beyond Campbell's Quest, I have found that four others are useful. Here they are in order of most to least useful for business audiences: Stranger in a Strange Land, Rags to Riches, Revenge, and Boy Meets Girl. Each has a distinctive structure and makeup, and the distinctions are important for presenters to understand. Let's take each one in turn.

The Quest is our most basic story of all.

The Quest is probably the most fundamental way we have of shaping our own experience and ways of relating to the world. In a Quest, a hero sets forth—often reluctantly—to achieve some difficult goal. Along the way, she encounters obstacles (dangers, enemies, roadblocks, and the like) that she has to overcome in order to reach the goal. She may acquire a mentor who helps at crucial moments with wisdom or advice to get around particular difficulties, or to close in finally on the real goal at journey's end.

The overwhelming emotional condition is hunger or longing for the goal. The hero may be reluctant at first, but eventually does get caught up in the need to reach the end, the point, the prize. The Holy Grail is one of our society's basic Quest stories. It is typical in nearly all respects—it has heroes, mentors, obstacles, and the like—except for one.

In the typical Quest, the hero achieves the goal and then returns to celebrate her victory and explain what she has achieved. In most tellings of the grail story, all the knights but one fail in the attempt to find the grail, and that knight often doesn't return, but rather goes straight up to heaven.

The shape of a Quest is thus essentially linear, unless it does involve a strong return or celebration. In that case, it acquires a kind of circularity. In other words, the hero returns, but in a different guise, or to a different place. One of the deep lessons of Quest stories is that you can't go home again—a cliché, to be sure, but precisely because there are so many stories that follow this form. The values that underlie the Quest story are pluck, determination, luck, courage in the face of overwhelming odds—in short, a celebration of the underdog.

The hero is not often valued for her expertise. That is usually left to the mentors. We admire the hero for winning despite all the difficulties that youth, inexperience, and hard terrain can throw in her path.

Quest stories work well for all kinds of business situations. Whether it is trying to reach some sales figures, or bring out a new product, or open a new plant, Quests are everywhere in modern corporate life.

For presentations about change, try Stranger in a Strange Land.

The hero of a Strange Land story is in a different pickle altogether. She's thrown into a new situation, literally a strange land or terrain. She doesn't know the local customs, the language, the rules, the path forward, or all of the above. Her emotional state is one of loss and confusion. Her goal is not necessarily to get to someplace, but rather to achieve knowledge, understanding, or competence in this strange new place.

Once again she may encounter mentors who help her find her bearings. But her primary struggle is to begin to achieve mastery after having all her mastery stripped away. Thus the essential structure of a Strange Land story is roughly circular. The best ones, indeed, involve a recognition at the end that the strange land is in fact not strange, but one you've known all along. *Planet of the Apes* (the original, not the remake) is thus the quintessential Strange Land story. When Charlton Heston sinks to his knees at the end of the movie, recognizing this strange ape-country for an America of the distant future (after seeing the Statue of Liberty half buried in the sand), the story has come full circle. Heston's character has not only *learned* the ways of this new land, but he now *knows* it, because he recognizes it. That is not to underestimate the importance of all the learning Heston's character has undergone while among the apes. That is indeed the heart of the Stranger in a Strange Land story, where most of the fun and the challenges lie—and therefore the interest.

Strange Land heroes can be experts in their own arcane knowledge. The values celebrated in these stories have to do with intelligence, quickness on your feet, the ability to improvise, coolness and poise, and learning.

Businesses that are trying to master a new marketplace, or to grow overseas, or to react to new competitive situations in familiar markets are involved in Stranger in a Strange Land stories.

In a materialistic age, there's always Rags to Riches.

Rags to Riches stories are linear. The hero begins in a state of privation, and by luck or hard work or some combination thereof wins security and riches. Power and fame can also be the prizes at the end of the rainbow and the story. The best Rags to Riches stories involve heroes who possess ordinary qualities and extraordinary luck. We can infer that, because these deep cultural stories usually have some form of an Everyman or Everywoman as the main character, we don't like to reward our heroes for their skill as much as for being in the right place at the right time and having the wit and luck to realize it, or at least to capitalize on it. If the hero were truly exceptional, we wouldn't be able to identify as readily with him or her.

The emotions involved are hunger, greed, loneliness, and alienation. The values associated with the story are similar to the Quest: pluck, grit, determination. And additionally, a few that are unique to this particular story: order, rationality, and hard (routine) work.

Entrepreneurs who aren't on quests are usually involved in Rags to Riches stories. They work well for small companies trying to grow big, and divisions of companies trying to get established. Quest stories have an end, so they have to be used with care. If you convince your listeners that they must achieve some goal, they will feel complete when they do so. The story, and their effort, will be over. It's why successful start-ups have such a hard time sustaining their energy after the first success is reached. The advantage of a Rags to Riches story is that it doesn't come to an abrupt end. Keeping and enjoying the riches can go on forever.

Hate is as strong as love, so you can also try Revenge.

Revenge stories are universal. We all love a good enemy. The structure of the story is linear, except in the variant in which a recognition of the true nature of the enemy forms the ending of the story, creating a kind of circularity. There's the wrong done to the hero, who loses everything, or almost everything, and then sets out to avenge the wrong. The best stories involve not only simple revenge, but also a psychological component that involves not being able to achieve revenge until you fully know or understand your enemy. *Star Wars* is an excellent example of this kind of Revenge tale. Luke Skywalker is not in a position to take his revenge against Darth Vader until he learns the full identity of his enemy. Then, of course, the nature of the revenge changes entirely as he learns that Vader is his father. It is in this psychological component of recognition that a sort of circularity is to be found.

The underlying emotion of the Revenge story is an interesting conundrum. There is of course the hero's anger and the villain's hatred. But both often end up confusingly close to love, once the recognition is achieved. Revenge stories are thus best understood as love stories gone wrong. For them to work, the feelings have to have the intensity of love.

The values of the Revenge story have to do with justice, right and wrong, the order of the community, and respect for individual human lives.

Many businesses (like Intel and every software company that takes on Microsoft) seem to have an affinity for Revenge stories. Whenever a company has a rival to take on (especially a bigger one), Revenge is a good story to invoke. We do love to see an underdog triumph over a larger enemy!

Finally, don't forget the power of love: Boy Meets Girl.

This story needs little explanation. The structure is again circular or elliptical, since the boy falls in love upon meeting the girl, loses the girl through misunderstanding or plot complication, and then finally wins her back in the end. Typically, though, the boy wins the girl by achieving a level of honesty or revelation that he hasn't had before. In comedic treatments of the story, for example, the boy will be concealing some appalling secret that, if revealed, could jeopardize the relationship. It is not until the secret is out and the complications are worked through that the two can get together. And the point is that they are both different because of the experience. The boy has learned (if the story is true to form) something about the importance of commitment and honesty. The girl has learned that her boy is not perfect, but is still worthy of love. Community values are expressed or reestablished.

Of course, for "boy" and "girl" we can substitute "any life form" in this enlightened age, but the basic circle of love, loss, and love reestablished cannot be violated for the story to be satisfying. The basic emotional state is love and longing. The values underlying the story have to do with the importance of community, trust, and honesty, and the twin polarities of loneliness and longing, happiness and satisfaction.

The modern business world is full of mergers, partnerships, joint ventures, and the like—all of which are potential love stories.

Relate stories to the audience's needs.

Those are the five mythic stories most applicable to presentations. How do they in fact relate specifically to public speaking and your developing presentation, which has so far been coming into focus around the audience's needs?

It's simple really. The audience needs to understand what you, the speaker, are up to as quickly as possible. As we've noted, taking in new information through the ear is hard work. So you want to orient your listeners as quickly as possible. You want to hook them with mythic stories that they know already, deeply and powerfully, from their cultural understandings developed over a lifetime. You want to frame the information you have to give in a persuasive package of fundamental Story.

And, of course, by drawing them in with these fundamental stories, you will increase their emotional investment in your presentation, as well as their retention of it.

A couple of examples:

Let's say you're making a presentation to the board about the new product you've got in the pipeline that's going to revolutionize the marketplace and lock up profits for your company for some time to come. There are just one or two little problems along the way—difficulties in production making it hard to achieve the volume you need, and quality control issues.

These are glitches, no more—if you're on a Quest. Then every roadblock becomes something to overcome, go around, or think your way past. The focus is on the goal, the grail, the successful product introduction. You will get there. It will be worth the effort. The team will make the necessary sacrifices to achieve the goal.

The point is to frame your briefing in these terms, with these overtones playing throughout the talk. It will be more effective if you don't say, "We're on a quest," but rather talk in terms of the conditions, features, and goals of a Quest. Your anecdotes can be miniature quests, or pieces of them, and your call to action at the end can be a stirring paean to enlist the team in the fun, with grand allusions to your favorite historical Quest, whether it's Biblical, or Greek, or a drive for some half-remembered pennant.

Or let's say you're explaining to the troops how the changing marketplace has rendered half of your services irrelevant. A combination of new regulation, new market entrants, and global paranoia is making it very difficult to figure out how to continue along the successful path of rising profits that has sustained your company so well in the past decade.

What you want to tell them is that although the world has changed, it will be the disciplined application of the basic formula for business success that launched the company to begin with that will help the team now. So while conditions are different, and it appears that a whole new set of rules should apply, it's really a matter of recognizing what hasn't changed in the mix in order to point the way toward success.

That's the classic Stranger in a Strange Land story. You're suddenly surrounded by unfamiliar terrain and the going is rough. So you take a deep breath and start to explore. As you get to know the new place you find yourself in, you gradually recognize that certain old skills will in fact stand you in very good stead. Other, newer habits you had picked up during your years of success need to be tossed away. It's time to get back to business basics.

Once again, you want to focus on the confusion first; that's the basic condition for a Strange Land story. Make it as disorienting as you can. Get lost in the new strange trees with your audience. Get them worked up with the confusion you've felt, and even the despair you've experienced as you watched the profit margins begin to erode and weren't sure what exactly to do about them.

Then, you move to the recognition, and the compelling reminder to your audience of the timeless truths with which the business began, as you point out the new clarity you've achieved about the road ahead. There is no Holy Grail, no endpoint here as in a Quest; what's needed is a constant return to the basics, an ongoing effort to stay disciplined, focused, and aware of the changing new conditions.

The frame's the thing.

Do you begin to get the idea? For virtually every human situation, one of these basic stories can help frame how we understand it. The virtue of the frame is that it orients the audience quickly and points the way forward to a particular kind of experience. Consciously framing your presentation in terms of one of these stories draws upon powerful cultural imperatives. Your audience will begin to think about the outcome of the product launch, or the new threats to the marketplace, or the merger, or the threat from Microsoft, and the like, in certain specific ways that allow you to enlist them wholeheartedly to bring about specific outcomes. They're programmed, in short, to think and act the way you want them to.

As you're giving the speech, you've now got another reason to listen to your audience. Because you'll want to watch for the moment when it "gets" the frame. You'll see audience members react viscerally—they'll start to smile, they'll lean forward, or they may just relax because they know they're in good hands and they're in for a good ride. You want to watch for that moment, because that's when you know that the audience is ready to listen to your persuasive argument. They're with you. You've won them over.

Remember

- People make meaning through the cultural stories we have all learned.

- Frame your presentation in terms of one of these powerful cultural stories.

- The Quest, Stranger in a Strange Land, Rags to Riches, Revenge, Boy Meets Girl—these are the most basic ones you can use in your presentations.

CHAPTER 7

Structure the Content

N OW IT'S TIME TO ACTUALLY ORGANIZE the content you're going to present to the audience.

We turn to the ancient Greeks once again for some basic wisdom here. The Greeks realized that you couldn't just deliver information; *you had to present it in terms that your audience was interested in.* They understood very well the need for an audience-centered presentation.

A classic example of this is the speeches in the *Iliad* that a group of envoys delivers to the inert Achilles, who has been sulking in his tent because the war has not been going to his liking. The problem the rest of the Greeks have is that without Achilles, they are being beaten easily by the Trojans. But they don't simply say to Achilles, "We're getting whipped, help!" That would

Thinking and presenting an idea in terms of your AUDIENCE

73

be putting the presentation together in terms of their problem, not Achilles'.

Instead, they realize that they have to appeal to Achilles' massive ego, so they talk about his contribution thus far in the most praiseworthy terms, as well as listing the prizes—riches, princesses, greater fame—that he will win if he will simply bestir himself. The whole point is that Achilles is feeling slighted and downcast, and they try to correct this situation.

Use the problem-solution structure to persuade your audience.

Achilles' ego aside, do you see the basic format the Greeks are working with here? It's the logical format known for centuries as *problem-solution*. Problem: Achilles is feeling depressed. Solution: Get him out to slaughter a bunch of Trojans. He'll feel better as soon as he's once again getting the glory he craves.

Besides "problematizing" the issues, there are also a number of other ways one can organize presentation material logically. For instance, you can reason:

- From cause to effect (if you do this, then that will happen)

- By definition (this is like that)

- By classification (this new phenomenon belongs to that familiar group)

- By authority (the experts say we should do this)

- By weighing probabilities (the odds are this will be successful)

- Inductively (having observed all these particulars, I derive this general rule)

- Deductively (using this general rule, I predict these particulars)

- By comparative advantages (you could do this, but that is better for the following reasons)

- From criteria to satisfaction (you want this, that will fulfill your needs)

- From general to specific (as a rule, this happens, so in that case, it will probably happen again)

- Using simple chronology (first this happened, then that)

- By eliminating options (you don't want to do this or that; thus, only the other alternative is left)

Each of these can work for organizing a presentation.

The real secret is to have a logical structure that is clear and transparent for the audience. Audiences like to feel that the speaker knows what she is doing; it's part of giving provisional authority to speakers, something that happens with every presentation. Authority is yours to lose, and you keep it with well-organized content and confident delivery. The problem-solution structure just usually happens to be the best way to organize the content in most persuasive speeches. That's because it puts the content of the presentation in an order and a context that the audience can easily digest. As I've noted, audiences begin by asking "Why?": Why should I grant provisional authority to the speaker in front of me? What will I get out of this speech if I do that? Stating a problem first answers that question right away, puts the audience at ease, and allows you to move on to the next crucial question, as we'll see.

The basic structure we're talking about is quite simple. You state a problem, and then you explain how to solve it. But here's what makes that simple formula powerful: *You state a problem that you know your listeners have.* Then, when you explain your solution, you'll have their interest.

Think of it this way: If you present a lot of information, you'll gain credibility—and lose the audience's interest. People simply can't remember enough information to make it worthwhile in a presentation. But if you solve an audience's problem, you'll gain its trust. And that trust is the beginning of a relationship, one that will allow you to move your audience, whether new friends or familiar colleagues, to action.

So the secret here is to think about the information you have, your expertise, not as a body of knowledge per se, but in terms of the audience. *What is the problem that the audience has for which my information is the solution?* That's the heart of the matter. Work out a good answer to that question, and you'll engage the audience powerfully every time.

The secret of persuasion is to respect your audience's need to make a decision.

Once you know what that problem is, you're in a position to win the one essential thing you need in order to succeed as a persuasive orator with an audience: trust. The best you'll ever do as long as you think of the audience as passive recipients of your wisdom, and your task as providing information, is establish credibility. That's not a bad thing; indeed, it's a minimal condition to succeed as a speaker, but it's not enough. You need to establish a trusting relationship with the audience, and you do that by solving their problems.

Now here's where it gets interesting. In order to solve this problem of the audience in a way that's audience-centered and that brings them along with you, *you need to respect their decision-making process.* Or to put it another way, your goal in a speech is to lead the audience through a decision-making process to solve a problem it has and for which you have the solution. Let's be very clear about this: You're going to provide the solution, although you may well get the audience to fill in some specifics, but you're going to lead the audience to that solution by respecting and following its decision-making process.

To make it plain how this process works, let's look at a concrete example. We'll take a straightforward business issue: declining earnings.

You're the division head. Earnings last quarter hurtled downward. You think you know how to turn the slide around in the second quarter, but it's going to require everyone working a little harder this quarter as well as a little smarter. You've got the smart idea. Now you just need to persuade your employees to work a little harder.

That's no easy task when everyone is already working 24/7/365, or pretty close to it. How can you motivate them to give a little more? You're facing them tomorrow at 9 A.M. What are you going to say?

The answer is, you're going to structure your speech so that it follows a universal human pattern: decision making. You're going to do that because just telling them isn't good enough. You're smart enough to know that unless your employees own the decision, they won't act on it.

Decision making involves five steps.

*This is a slightly modified
Monroe's Motivated Sequence*

Decision making follows five clear steps, and your presentation needs to lead your audience through them. Speech making is a linear process—it happens in real time. Your audience needs to go on the decision-making journey with you. Each step has to happen at the right time.

The first step in decision making is to realize that there is a problem and understand how it relates to you. Without that realization, there is no need for the audience to commit to a change. So you'll begin by getting your audience's attention by telling a very brief story that illustrates and frames the problem. What will your story be? It should be something that comes immediately out of your particular situation. Perhaps you've had a conversation with a disgruntled employee or customer? Or a positive experience with a rival's product?

Second, you'll dive into a thorough and honest analysis of the situation. That exercise corresponds to the fact-gathering that people undertake when they know they have a problem. What are the causes of the downturn? What are all the ins and outs of your supply chain? What does your customer satisfaction data look like? The key here is not to pull punches. Tell it to 'em straight. Don't point fingers. But don't avoid painful truths.

Third, the good part: Present your solution. If it's going to be controversial, lay out three alternatives and tell, in order, why each one won't work. Then describe your favored solution, and describe its pitfalls, too. The point is, after all, to walk them through the decision-making process, so if there are other obvious alternatives, and pitfalls to your own, don't avoid them. If you do, the audience will start creating them at the water cooler after the talk, and all your hard work will be for nothing. I call this the *residues method*, by the way, and I'll have more to say about it a bit later on. If it's not desperately controversial, then just present your solution simply and straightforwardly.

Fourth, you'll spell out the benefits of the choice that you want them to make. The key issue here is to help them to visualize the good things ahead. If you dwell on the negatives at this point, you'll simply inspire them to gloom, not action. So don't threaten. Rather, help them over the difficult hurdle of actually making a decision by painting alluring pictures of possible (but real) success that awaits them. Profit sharing? Big year-end bonuses? Continued employment? Lay out the rewards for all to see.

This is good

Finally, you need to get them started on the action that you want them to take. Give them a small, easy step to take right there, in the room. You'll find that it makes the follow-up steps seem much more possible. Once people have made a decision and taken a modest step toward realizing the benefits of that decision, they've done the hardest work. The rest may take all of the second quarter and involve a lot of long hours, but it's relatively easy by comparison.

What might that small step look like? It could be creating a "to do" list for each department or group. It could be filling out a diagnostic exercise that shows where departmental opportunities for growth exist. It could take the form of a commitment to a series of steps to be taken later. If it involves that sort of abstract commitment, make sure that you have the audience do something physical, such as write down their individual goals on a 3 x 5 card or the like.

You can order people to act, but the harder you push, the more push-back you'll get. Rather, the smart speaker leads her employees down the decision-making path, letting them do all the hard work of commitment themselves. If you do it right, you'll have a team of people who can't wait to get to work turning those numbers around.

So that's how you tie a great presentation to the audience's need to make a decision to act in real time. Begin by helping the people in front of you realize the need exists. Then gather the facts for them. Then lay out the solution, describe the benefits, and give them a modest action to take right there in the room.

That's the system in a nutshell. We've begun with the ancient Greeks, but left them behind by tying their structural analysis of a persuasive speech with the audience's need to follow a decision-making process. This coupling is essential if your presentation is to have any lasting effect. It's a key piece of what I mean by listening to your audience. It's a matter of showing them the respect due real people whom you genuinely want to move, to persuade to action. You don't do that by dazzling them, or by podium antics, or by flashy PowerPoint slides (least of all those!). You do it by taking them with you on a journey that honors their thought processes and their need to have both intellect and emotion fed in the work that they do.

To see whether or not you're successful in the journey, listen to your audience after you've begun to present your solution. If the people in the room buy in to your answer, you'll notice that their questions will take the form of "how?" rather than "why?" Questions like: How do I do this? How can we get started? Not, Why is this the best method? Why aren't other companies trying this?

Because it is so important, let's look at each step in the decision-making journey in more detail in chapter 8, with special focus on the last step—the action step—which generally gives speakers the most trouble.

Remember

- A persuasive speech sets out the problem first, then the solution.

- Audiences want speeches that have a clear, simple, logical structure.

- Ask yourself, what is the problem the audience has for which my information is the solution?

- A successful speaker wins the audience's trust by solving its problems.

- A good speech takes its audience on a journey from why to how.

- A persuasive speech follows the audience's decision-making process.

Lincoln Gives the Best Speech Ever

The greatest short speech ever given is Lincoln's Gettysburg Address. In just over 250 words—roughly two minutes' talking at normal speed—Lincoln put the Civil War and the battle of Gettysburg in the context of the nation's constitutional history and proposed that the best way to honor those who had fallen in that terrible fight would be to finish the work of preserving the union in a "new birth of freedom."

It's a masterpiece of concision and restrained pathos. But it has another lesson to teach us as well: It's brilliantly organized for maximum persuasive effect, using the problem-solution method described in this chapter. Herewith is Lincoln's model, followed by three variations to use when the circumstances of the speech dictate an alternate approach.

First, frame a situation—hook the audience.

Lincoln hooks the audience by eloquently describing the situation at hand. The Civil War, the battle of Gettysburg, and the dedication ceremony are all mentioned in crisp, clear phrases. But note that Lincoln actually starts his speech with an apparent look backward. "Fourscore and seven years ago our fathers brought forth on this continent a new nation, conceived in liberty and dedicated to the proposition that all men are created equal."

Why start here? Precisely because Lincoln wishes to frame his eulogy in the context of the constitutional history of the country. He's telling us what is at stake—our personal freedoms and the life of the country. The story that Lincoln is telling doesn't begin with the battlefield, but rather back at the creation of the United States itself. In this fashion, he raises the ante of the day well beyond the battle—as grim as that was—and sets the lives of the soldiers who perished against the continuation of the country.

The lesson for anyone designing a presentation today is to be very clear about what the story is that you wish to tell. Begin at the beginning of *that* story. But you can only do that if you know exactly what you want the audience to get out of the speech. You must frame, or define, the situation precisely with the end in mind.

Then give the audience a complication or problem.

Next Lincoln pulls the rhetorical rug out from under his audience by telling them: "But, in a larger sense, we cannot dedicate, we cannot consecrate, we cannot hallow this ground." He adds a complication to his description of the current situation. He creates a problem. Why can't we dedicate this ground? After all, that was the ostensible point of the occasion. Thus, he propels his story forward by making the audience wonder how indeed they can accomplish the consecration they're all expecting.

This is the key step in a persuasive speech. It's the moment at which you either take your listeners with you, or lose them for good. Lincoln succeeded because his rhetorical move was unexpected. It was exactly opposite to the bromides about honoring the dead the audience might have reasonably anticipated. The best problem statements accomplish this reversal by taking your listeners somewhere they weren't quite expecting to go. In this way, your speech is not only interesting, but it also demonstrates that you're worth listening to because you have insight into the situation that no one else has.

Conclude by offering a solution and suggesting an action.

Instead of merely grieving at the battlefield, Lincoln suggests, we would better honor the dead by finishing the work they began. "It is for us the living, rather, to be dedicated here to the unfinished work which they who fought here have thus far so nobly advanced." In other words, let's get on with winning the war and putting the country back together.

This solution points the assembled listeners toward the action Lincoln desires them to take. "That we here highly resolve that these dead shall not have died in vain, that this nation, under God, shall have a new birth of freedom, and that government of the people, by the people, for the people, shall not perish from the earth." It is a rhetorical action ("we resolve"), but an action nonetheless, to maintain this experiment in democracy on earth. All good speeches close with an action for the audience, either actual or rhetorical. The action may be small, but it should be significant.

Lincoln's insight was to take this "problem-solution" structure and apply it to a eulogy, something generally considered to be an ornamental speech more suited to flowery phrases than tight logic. He made his case brilliantly; he persuaded his audience to offer up the deaths of the soldiers of Gettysburg on the altar of the living Republic. But could he have organized the speech in other ways as well? What other organizational formats are possible for presentations?

Present a decision to be made.

Had Lincoln wanted to present a series of options for the audience to choose among, he would have proceeded a little differently. First, he would have begun by defining the problem: "We cannot dedicate, we cannot consecrate, we cannot hallow this ground." Then he would have developed a list of criteria for evaluating a series of possible solutions to this problem. Next, he would have listed all the relevant solutions, and evaluated them against his criteria. He would pick the best solution and suggest ways to implement it, discussing the various issues that might arise during implementation. Lincoln, of course, wanted to give his listeners one option only, precisely because he was so afraid they were apt to choose others.

This format—definition, criteria, solutions, evaluation, selection, implementation—is effective for helping or guiding an audience to choose among options. Rhetorically, you should present the option you intend the audience to favor at the end of your list, because audiences tend to remember best things they hear last.

Deliver bad news.

If Lincoln had considered his task to be one of delivering bad news— the terrible toll of death on the battlefield—he would have begun by describing briefly the background to the immediate situation that gave rise to the bad news. It's the usual way that eulogies are begun. This device gives the audience time to prepare for the blow. Foreshadowing helps, but you don't want to make them wait too long. The audience will resent bad news delivered in the middle or end of a long speech, because it seems deceptive. Thus, it's important to give the bad news directly after the ground is readied. Then you may present various options for the audience to take in responding to the news, and follow the decision-making structure for the rest of the presentation. Or you can follow the last structure, one useful for imparting information.

Impart information.

Finally, had Lincoln intended only to present important information to his audience, he would have followed a general presentation model that works particularly well when time is limited and you want to make sure you've covered all the rhetorical bases. First, outline the situation. Then, describe your specific role in it. Next, tell what action you took and what the results were. Finally, offer your analysis or recommendations for the path forward. This format is useful for updating your boss or the board on a work in progress. When you have such a situation well in hand, and you don't really want to reopen the decision-making process, this structure works well. In Lincoln's case, persuasion was called for, because he had to unite an uncertain populace behind him.

These four structures—problem-solution, decision making, bad news delivery, and information imparting—cover virtually every presentation one could make. Your bias should always be toward using the problem-solution structure. It is the most interesting for audiences, it involves them most readily, and it is the best method of persuading audiences. And if you're not persuading them, what are you doing in front of them?

CHAPTER 8

Make the Journey

LEADING YOUR AUDIENCE ON THE important journey to a decision—to changing your listeners' minds—is not an easy task. There are many ways to go wrong, and many ways to lose your audience. By looking at the steps along the way in more detail, we can avoid some of the pitfalls that so often trap naïve speakers.

A good hook frames the terms of your presentation memorably.

First, you orient your audience. You frame the problem. We think in terms of stories, as I've said; it's our birthright. It's how our brains work. So you need to begin by telling them a quick story, anecdote, or parable that sets up the presentation you're going to give them. One, in other words, that tells the same story in miniature that you're going to tell throughout the presentation. It should touch on the emotional as well as the intellectual journeys you are going to take your audience on. It should be based on one of the five stories I described in chapter 6.

By the way, don't think that you have to tell a joke. That's one of the oldest bits of advice in the trade, and it has helped many a speech fall flat within the first few minutes of beginning. The simple reason is that most people don't tell jokes very well. What's more, they tell them worse when they're at their most nervous. It's a likely recipe for disaster. Take one nervous person, force him to tell a joke to a roomful of strangers, and then make him give a presentation once the joke has fallen flat and he's facing a roomful of unhappy listeners. Does this sound like a good idea?

The best way to open a presentation is with a parable—a story with a point or moral. Make the parable simple, honest, and emotional. Make it personal, if possible. Also, tell it in less than three minutes. The point should cover, in a general way, the direction you're headed during the speech.

The key to successful storytelling, especially in the case of parables, is ruthless elimination of all extraneous information. Consider the following.

> *There was this guy, a farmer. He lived in Iowa, in the western part of state, where the land is flat—though, of course, it's flat everywhere in Iowa, isn't it? In fact, it's a square, flat state. Sometimes for fun on a Saturday night, they tell me, Iowans get in the car and drive until they find a bump in the road and they get out and look at it. Then they go get all their friends, and they all come out and look at it. Iowa is a windy state, too, they tell me, and a lot of farmers, this one included, have put up windmills to sell power to the power companies and earn a little extra money. It's tough making a living as a farmer. Anyway, this farmer planted a number of mixed crops, varying the crops in rotation so as to get the most out of his land. Sometimes, then,*

he planted 40 percent alfalfa, 40 percent wheat, and 20 percent corn.
Other times he increased the amount of corn to 50 percent, and de-
creased the alfalfa and wheat to 25 percent each. Well, one year he
planted in a strong breeze, and the seed blew all around and some
landed on the edges of the field where the road went. The birds ate all
that. And some landed in the worst part of the land, a rocky part
where the wind had eroded the soil, and that didn't grow. It was only
the seeds that landed in the good land that grew.

Did you get the point? Probably not; it was buried in irrelevant detail. Was it about how dull Iowa is? Or about wind farming? Or crop rotation? Or where seed is likely to grow? You may
think to yourself, who would tell a story like that? But when we
tell stories about ourselves, we seem to find it necessary to fix
unimportant bits of data with a kind of certainty that drives the
audience mad and means nothing to them.

Instead, tell a parable like an expert does.

A sower went out to sow his seed, and as he sowed, some fell along the
path, and was trodden under foot, and the birds of the air devoured
it. And some fell on the rock; and as it grew up, it withered away,
because it had no moisture. And some fell among thorns; and the
thorns grew with it and choked it. And some fell into good soil and
grew, and yielded a hundredfold.

—Matthew 13:4–9

Note how all the detail is stripped away except that which is
absolutely crucial to the point. Note also that the moral, or point,
is contained—but not explicitly stated—in the last sentence. Finally, note that the subject of the parable is carefully chosen to
connect well with Jesus' audience, which was rural and understood farming.

Those are the key points to remember in telling a successful
parable: no irrelevant detail, an implicit moral at the end, and a
topic that the audience can understand.

Think of the problem as an issue that the audience has that you have the information to solve.

Once you've hooked your audience with a good story, you're ready to work on the full statement of the problem. Understand that there are fundamentally two kinds of problems: one the audience already knows about, and one that they're either not fully persuaded of, or is news to them. If your problem is of the second kind, then you're going to have to work harder persuading the audience that you're talking about the problem they need to worry about, right here, right now.

Either way, the first third to half of the speech should be spent outlining this problem. Remember, you're taking the audience on both an intellectual and emotional journey. It takes time. Speeches happen in real time; they are linear. That means that you have to bring the audience along with you. You have to allow them time to feel the emotions you're talking about. If you want them to get worried about the state of the business, then you have to paint a disturbing picture and actually let them feel worried for a while. Don't bring them out of it. Don't offer the solution right away. You want the audience to feel uncomfortable. If you don't, your speech will have no power to move the audience as you begin to offer your solution.

That's why you have to listen to the audience. It's your job as a speaker to know how they're doing, both emotionally and intellectually. As you take them on the journey you have prepared, you have to test regularly how the trip is going for them.

Your goal is to lead your audience down into the valley of despair before taking them up the mountainside of hope. One example of a real master at taking an audience through this journey is the strategy guru Gary Hamel. His descriptions in the first half of his speeches (of the tragic state that his audience is mired in) are masterpieces of anecdote, detail, fact, statistic, and insightful analysis all worked together in a patchwork quilt of persuasion that leaves his listeners, typically Fortune 1000 executives, in no doubt as to what dinosaurs they have become, doomed to extinction. His speeches bear close study.

Complete the journey by taking your audience into the promised land of your solution.

Once you're quite convinced that the audience has absorbed the problem and become thoroughly agitated, it's time to bring forth your solution and lead them out of despair into hope. Very roughly, this exercise should take up the second half of the speech. Here's where you outline the solution and then fill in the details with a true vision of how the solution could benefit the audience in front of you.

It's important to be concrete about the benefits that your solution will have for the audience. Better yet, get the audience involved in figuring out what those benefits are. Give them a case study and let them work out what the possible solutions might be.

Depicting the benefits of your solution—in concrete terms for a specific audience—is so important that the modern version of this ancient Greek speech outline gives it a step of its own. This modern version is called the Monroe sequence or model, after the person who developed it, Alan H. Monroe, and it draws upon insights into the psychological makeup of the audience and the nature of speech making. Basically, it's the point that, because speeches are linear and inefficient ways of taking in information, it's hard work for an audience to think concretely about benefits to itself. You need to help the audience. Hence the "benefits" step. It's the point where you bring the audience into the new world of your solution by painting a compelling picture of all the positive things that will accrue to the audience if it goes along with you. Hamel, again, does this very well. He describes the antithesis to the dinosaur he depicts at the beginning of his talks: a flexible, fast, customer-centric corporation that can outpace the competition and satisfy the marketplace every time.

If the topic is very controversial, use the *residues* method.

Sometimes the topic you're covering is controversial. In that case, the best way to ensure that the audience will consider the alternative you're offering is to use a variant of the problem-solution method called the residues method.

The residues method is so named because after presenting the problem, you don't immediately jump to your solution. Rather, you present a series of alternatives, together with the typical objections to those solutions, until you've fairly considered and rejected all the options except your own. Then, you take your own position as the "residue" left after all the other options are gone.

Let's look at a quick example. President Bush used precisely this method during his speech on stem-cell research in August 2001. He faced considerable challenges in getting a nation interested in this rather esoteric debate on the frontiers of medical science. For starters, we live in an era of passionate, partisan speaking. Turn on any TV talk show, and you're liable to watch the often less-than-edifying spectacle of public figures interrupting each other rudely as they sling distortions, half-truths, and outright lies at one another. The nature of the medium, indeed, calls for hot tempers and simple messages. If you can't get the idea out in a twelve-second or eight-second sound bite, then TV isn't interested. And it had better be emotional, or it won't hold the tube's attention.

The result is the oft-noted "dumbing down" of American public rhetoric. Important political issues of the day have been reduced to simple "either-or" positions, greatly diminishing the chances of any useful debate. So anxious are public figures to get their fifteen minutes of attention that they would prefer to spend it shouting than actually entering into a dialogue with their opponents that might move the debate forward.

That's what President Bush was up against. He responded with a rhetorically elegant, thoughtful speech that provided a textbook illustration of the residues method.

The president needed to make a decision either to allow stem-cell research to go forward with federal support or to stop federal spending in this area. Either way, he risked alienating voters on one side of the issue or the other—not a place most presidents would relish finding themselves in.

So Bush reached back to ancient Greek tradition and used a strategy that anyone faced with divided opinion on a hot topic can use effectively.

What you do is first lay out the question under debate, as neutrally as possible. Then you take up the possible answers, one by one, that have already been put forward. Once again, the idea is to present the opposing viewpoints as fairly as possible. This is essential, or else the various partisans will not feel that they have been heard.

As you describe each answer, you raise the problems with that answer. Bush did this. He described the position of those who favor stem-cell research because of the enormous potential benefit for curing some of our most deadly and intractable diseases. And he raised the problems with that position, that it involved working with cells that had come from discarded human embryos.

Bush also took up the position of those who favor no research at all and looked at the objections to that position, including the need not to fetter research, and for America not to fall behind globally in the biotech race, as well as the argument that the embryos in question were by and large already discarded anyway.

Finally, Bush announced his own, Solomon-like decision: to allow work with already harvested stem cells, but not to fund (publicly) any research from cells harvested after the day of the speech. Thus, this position was framed as the residue left when all the other positions were discussed and eliminated.

While extremists were not of course delighted with the solution

Bush proposed, there was surprisingly widespread support for a position that had not been articulated widely before. Because Bush carefully worked through the possible answers to the difficult question of public funding for stem-cell research, the public and the various partisans were able to feel that at least Bush had listened carefully to many voices on the subject and had thoughtfully developed his own answer.

That's what the residues method can do. Use it when your topic is similarly controversial and your audience polarized.

Finally, finish your presentation with the help of the audience.

Whether your topic is controversial or not, the description of your solution and its resulting benefits are really just preparation for the most important point in the outline: the action step. Here is where you win or lose the hearts, the energy, the commitment of the audience in front of you. The idea is that you get your audience to do something *with you*, something that might be described as the first step in the journey of commitment and change that you want them to take.

For years, speech instructors told their students, "tell 'em what you're going to say, say it, and tell 'em what you said." While this repetitive method certainly had the benefit of hammering points home, the problem with it is that audiences know what's coming. As soon as you say, "What I'm going to talk about today is . . . " half the audience stops listening. They figure that they're going to hear it again anyway. The other half listens hard so that they don't have to pay much attention during the talk itself. Then, at the end, when you say, "In summary, what I've said today is . . . " three-quarters of the audience is packing up, checking their schedules, text messages, even e-mail, or literally heading out the door. You've lost them. Given that the last thing an audience hears from you is the most important—because it's the part that's most likely to be remembered—why squander those moments on something that the audience will deliberately tune out?

So don't do it. Don't summarize. Instead, give them a call to action.

Good politicians have always instinctively recognized this need to stir an audience to action at the end. Their calls to action are often rhetorical, but they are calls to action nonetheless. President Kennedy, near the end of his inaugural address, famously said, "And so, my fellow Americans, ask not what your country can do for you—ask what you can do for your country." And, a moment later, somewhat less famously, "My fellow citizens of the world, ask not what America will do for you, but what together we can do for the freedom of man."

The proof that this call was a powerful one lies in the simple fact that the Peace Corps began with those words, and has led thousands of American youths to serve its mission all over the globe ever since.

That speech changed the world.

Note that political action steps are often just rhetorical. That's because politicians typically want the engagement that comes from a good speech without any specific response beyond positive feelings from their constituents. Most modern political leadership is conducted by polling, and all that's really required of the citizen is her acquiescence when the pollsters call. Sometimes, of course, they want the constituents' votes. Then the action steps tend to get a bit more pointed, and the rhetoric more harsh.

But businesspeople need something a little stronger. When you're making a presentation to your employees and the survival of the company hangs in the balance, you need those people to get up and do something real after you've finished talking. You want that motivation to last for more than a few minutes after you've concluded. And, of course, you want more than a few of your listeners to jump on the moving train.

The only way to ensure that you'll get this kind of real response from your audience is to give them an action step with some real action in it. By that I mean, *get the audience actually to do something there in the room at the end of your presentation.*

A typical one in a corporate setting is to get the audience to design the path forward after the solution you've proposed. So you tell them in broad strokes how to achieve year-to-year earnings growth, but let them set the unit goals or strategies to achieve the endpoint you've set out for them.

A Q&A session is not an action step.

A quick note about something that often gets used instead of a good action step: Q&A, or questions and answers. This format that has been around for a long time, and everyone uses it, but have you ever thought about its drawbacks? A Q&A session doesn't allow you to end the presentation with your strongest point. You leave the ending up to the last question, in effect. So in fact, you have little idea or control about what the ending—the most important thing the audience will hear—will be.

To be sure, some speakers return to their theme at the end of the Q&A session, in effect giving a brief speech after taking a few questions. This method does avoid the most obvious problems that a Q&A session presents. But it doesn't get around the fact that most people in the audience will be tuned out at this point. Remember, only one person asked the last question. That means that you only know for sure that one person in the audience is interested in the answer you're about to give. If you follow that up with concluding remarks, you may have to work hard to get the audience's attention and then deal with their resentment at being slipped a little more work to do just when they thought they were free.

Of course, some Q&A sessions are much, much more destructive than what I've just sketched out. Sometimes an angry or aggressive questioner will rattle you with a series of hostile accusations disguised as questions. Sometimes a bore will go on and on with a pointless question (or worse, no question at all) until everyone in the room forgets all your hard work in a concentrated desire to kill the bore. You can earn big points with an audience at that point by deftly shutting the bore down, but once again, that's all your listeners will remember. Your speech will be entirely lost in the shuffle.

So here's a radical thought: Don't do a Q&A. What to do instead? Take questions as they come up throughout. Now, to be sure, this method has its challenges. You need to be extremely comfortable in your talk, for one thing, so that you can stop and start it without losing momentum. You need to be very good handling audience responses so that you don't allow a question to derail you. And you need to know how to answer a question without giving away some upcoming part of your talk.

But changing the Q&A session to continuous audience response ties the audience in much more closely to the progress of the speech. It gives your listeners the impression that they are involved in the creation of the speech, as well as its shape and flow. And they think that you are a more responsive speaker than those who make them wait for a Q&A session. Better all around. It's audience-centered speaking.

Doing away with Q&A also allows you to create a strong action step that gets your audience involved, and to end on that very high note. What should you get your audience to do? The answer is, of course, different for every speech. But a couple of broad categories of thought will be useful here. Overall, try to think of a relatively easy action they could undertake that represents the first thing you would want them to do when they are back in their offices the next day and beginning to change the world for you.

Another way to think of it is to ask yourself what kind of commitment you want them to make. Is it to think differently? Then you want them to act out the first step in that changed thought process. Is it to work differently? Then you want them to make a commitment that will take them to the first bend in the road toward that new way of working. Is it to relate to the people around them differently? Then ask them to turn to their neighbors and get started.

Indeed, the fearless presenter can get the audience involved at any stage of the presentation. The action step is the essential place for audience involvement, but you can have audiences help articulate both the problem and the solution steps of your talk, as long as you're not giving the audience something that's too difficult to do on the spot.

In chapter 9 we'll look more closely at how to involve the audience.

Remember

- Use a parable to frame your presentation and orient the audience.

- State a problem the audience has for which your information is the solution.

- Use the residues method for particularly contentious topics.

- Help the audience picture the benefits of the solution you have given them.

- Rather than doing a Q&A, close by getting the audience to take an action step.

CHAPTER 9

Involve the Audience

YOU'RE READY TO COMPLETE YOUR preparation of the content of your speech by thinking about how to get the audience involved, especially during the action step.

It helps to talk about a few categories. Broadly speaking, in my experience, there are four good ways to involve your audience.

1. **TEACH:** Get the audience to take what they've learned and test it against someone else, or coach someone else in their development. Get them to pledge something to their neighbors—a commitment to a new form of behavior, or some longer-term goals.

2. **TELL A STORY:** Get the audience members to weave their personal stories into the larger one that the speaker

has just told. Case studies work well in this context. You can break the audience up into small groups, get them to tell each other their stories, and then collect them in some format for reporting back to the whole group.

3. PLAY: Get the audience to compete or play in some way to make the point of the talk real, either as individuals or in small groups. A debate is a good form of play, and you can have the audience coach and judge as well as debate.

4. DESIGN: Get your audience to design a specific path forward, or next steps, in the general journey you've begun them on. Diagnostic exercises, such as a series of questions designed to elicit cost-cutting options, are particularly good here.

Over the years, I've designed hundreds of action steps and other moments of audience participation for businesspeople to use with audiences all over the world. They can take many forms within these four categories, but they must be relevant to the speech and useful for the audience. In addition, they should be possible for the audience to complete in the time allotted.

Get your audience involved throughout the speech.

There are many tactics to use to involve the audience. You can have questionnaires and self-tests prepared. You can have them stand up and testify. You can have them undertake small group activities. You can even select individuals, as long as you find ways to make it clear that they represent the whole. There are no rules here except one: *Whatever you get the audience to do must reinforce in some way your elevator speech.*

Let's focus on the action step for a moment, remembering that the principles at work here apply to audience participation throughout the speech. How long should the action step last? How complicated should it be? How much can you actually get the audience to do? There are as many answers to these questions as there are speeches.

If you've done your job right, the audience is full of pent-up active energy. They can't wait to get working on the "how" because you've taken them on a powerful emotional journey, they know "why" they need to act, and they're ready to get started. They're waiting for you to give them a chance to give some of that energy back. When this happens, it is one of the most exciting and rewarding moments a speaker ever experiences—and you can make it happen every time you give a speech.

Teach your audience to commit to change.

I worked once with a human resources professional who was asked to give a speech at a big conference of human resources folks, with something like three thousand people in attendance. She was following Elie Wiesel and Andrew Young, two powerful speakers, and it was intimidating. She wanted to talk about the importance of realizing your life goals and not settling for less than your best effort. It's a fine theme, but it requires something real to bring it to life and to make it more than a cliché. When I challenged her to create something audience-centered, with a powerful action step at the end to raise the speech out of the realm of nice pieties, her reaction was quite reasonably skeptical. "How can I control three thousand people? How can I get them to do something? How can I make it meaningful?" she asked.

In our work together we uncovered a story that became the heart of the speech. It was a Quest story, and quite real—and heartbreaking. It was about her father's determination to see his daughter achieve her dream and his: completing her Ph.D. before he died of cancer. She told the story in a beautifully effective way, and enough time had gone by that she could tell it without weeping. She could be real, in other words, but she was not in the first flush of grief, which would have made her audience uncomfortable.

As she drew near the end of her speech, she asked the people in the audience to make a commitment right there and then to a life goal they had always wanted to achieve but had not yet managed to make the time for. Earlier she had distributed a simple prop: 3 x 5 cards. She asked her listeners to write the goals down on the cards, and then turn to a neighbor and explain their goals to them, as a further commitment. The explosion in energy as the audience undertook this process was extraordinary, and a number of audience members afterward told the speaker that they had exchanged e-mails, phone numbers, and addresses with the people around them, forming instant support groups to help each other realize their dreams.

The speech was rated more highly than either of the two by Wiesel or Young, both excellent speakers in their own right. For a long time afterward, she heard from members of the audience who took it upon themselves to keep her informed of their progress toward realizing their life goals.

She changed the world. That's a successful speech.

Note how simple this was to carry out. All it took was courage, a heartfelt personal story, and 3 x 5 cards. The rest was up to the audience.

It's important to realize that this action step was suited to the speaker, the occasion, and the audience. It wouldn't necessarily work anywhere else. You need to design your own. But this one should give you some ideas.

It's also important to realize that, while this was a keynote speech to a large audience, the technique—the action step—will work just as well with smaller groups. In fact, with smaller groups you will want to use a more informal approach that gets the audience doing more for you rather than less. Don't wait for the end to get the audience involved, especially in a small group. Start early and often.

Now, the foregoing is an example of "teaching," and it works best in this kind of setting, where your job as speaker is to create an inspirational context to allow the audience to make a commitment to a new course of some kind.

It's worth looking at the other three kinds of audience involvement listed at the beginning of the chapter so you can get a sense of the variety and power of these ways of interacting with an audience.

Toys help tell a story.

My favorite example of how well the "tell a story" approach can work is a presentation a consultant gave on the difficulties of merging corporate cultures. We had presents wrapped and placed on the chairs of the audience members. Everyone was instructed not to open them until the signal was given.

The speaker began by presenting the facts of the case: the merger of the two toy companies Mattel and Fisher-Price. On the face of it, the merger should have been an easy win for Mattel, the acquiring company. Both were highly successful toy companies, with substantial profits and reasonably good historical growth patterns. But closer inspection revealed some deep-seated problems. Mattel had coasted on the success of Barbie for years. In fact, half of Mattel's revenue came from Barbie—a dangerous overdependency on one toy. Part of the impetus for the merger, indeed, was to bring other successful product lines into the mix. Mattel had had little success in attempting to create other toy "hits" like Barbie, indicating a weak product development process in an industry that thrives on perpetual product innovation.

The real issues, though, had to do with the different cultures of the two companies. Mattel focused on the preteen market with Barbie and action figures whereas Fisher-Price sold preschool toys with simple plastic shapes and primary colors—barnyards, school buses, houses with families in them. The point was that the culture of each company mirrored the toys they produced. The teenage heart of Mattel's appeal was deeply alien to the people of Fisher-Price, who were concerned with education and the mental growth of children. Mattel's attitude was much edgier, as its toys strove to meet the needs of pubescent and near-pubescent kids. What looked on the surface like an easy merger was in fact a potential train wreck as the two product development teams brought their different assumptions together in an effort to work as a team.

The speaker presented this puzzle to the audience and solicited their suggestions for the first critical actions of the combined company postmerger. What should the new toy company do first? What kind of merger should Mattel attempt—a friendly one? Or one in which the goal was to eliminate Fisher-Price thinking as quickly as possible, not to mention employees? The speaker asked the audience to form small groups and work out what the critical next steps should be.

The audience responded with enthusiasm, and came up with a number of suggestions, one of which (as the presenter guessed) was to get the combined company to work designing a new line of toys that took the best thinking of the two individual firms.

The presenter then turned that question back to the audience. What should that new line of toys look like? At that point, the audience was asked to unwrap the presents, which turned out to be a mixture of Mattel and Fisher-Price toys. The cultural problems inherent in the two wildly different approaches to toys became visceral and obvious. Amid much enthusiastic response, laughter, and even horse trading of toys, the small groups grappled with the issue of combining the companies symbolically through a combined toy line.

The point was not what they came up with, although one group did suggest a line of toys that was quite similar to one that Mattel in fact attempted later. The point for our audience was simply to get a visceral sense of the difficulties involved in merging even seemingly similar companies. The case study action step was the perfect work for the audience to undertake in order to get a good sense of the problem and to begin to work out some ways to craft solutions for different kinds of mergers, which the presenter was able to highlight in a quick wrap-up at the close of the presentation.

Audiences love "play" competitions.

Information technology executives are not typically known for their public demonstrations of exuberance, but I once saw a group of them cheering their enthusiasm. The talk leading up to this extraordinary outburst involved some research on how to survive what was an increasingly difficult job. Businesspeople often don't understand new technology, yet they need it (and need to spend money on it) to survive and flourish in the business world today. On the IT side, the employees feel like devotees of a misunderstood and persecuted cult. They are derided as nerds, and yet most nontechnical employees won't take the time to learn even half of what they need to know to be able to function in a technology-saturated world. Caught in the middle, trying to explain one side to the other, is the chief information officer.

The speaker had developed three models for how a CIO might behave successfully, and rather than just tell the audience about it, he opted to get three volunteers to respond to a posed problem they might face as an imaginary CIO. He divided the audience into three groups, and had them each coach a volunteer according to one of the three models about what he should say during the interview that formed the basis of the role-playing. Note that the audience wasn't inventing the three models; that would have been too much to ask of them. The presenter had already described the three for them. What they did was fill in the models with specific scripting—words for the volunteers to say. Incidentally, putting a third of the audience to work supporting the volunteer also made that job much less stressful, and made it easier to get volunteers. It was the group, rather than an individual, that had its credibility on the line.

The three volunteers did their jobs well, and the audience was invited to respond with applause for each, to determine which approach was the best. Of course, each third of the audience shamelessly clapped and yelled for its own volunteer; that was expected. The point wasn't really to determine a winner, but to get the audience to consider some alternatives and to use its creative power to invest in new ways of thinking about the CIO's role. The results, not only in terms of enthusiasm in the moment, but in terms of the thoughtful comments received by the presenter for weeks afterward, more than repaid the risks involved in the presentation.

When in doubt, get the audience to design a solution.

I've worked with many change agents, but the most revolutionary thinker I've worked with is a self-styled "corporate outlaw" named Chris Turner. She has a book out with the intriguing title of *All Hat and No Cattle: Tales of a Corporate Outlaw* that describes her efforts to make change at the ground level at Xerox. Chris "got" action steps right away, since her central idea is that people hate change but love to remodel. In other words, if you can get them to do it, it will go well. If it's pushed on them, it won't work. In fact, the only real difficulty I had with Chris was that she wanted to make the entire speech an action step, doing away with virtually all the need to talk to the audience at all before they were put to work. For one series of speeches, basically a kick-off event to be repeated several times in various locales around the country, we talked about self-diagnostic tools (which revealed some of the areas of greatest resistance to change) as a way of getting the audience to document just how difficult it was to change and how far the organization had to go. But in the end, Chris's ambition extended much further, and the kickoff events became real first steps in launching change initiatives right there, with substantial work being done before the speech was over.

Most speakers don't have the comfort level with themselves and the belief in the audience to do what Chris was willing to do: Get out of the way and trust the audience to figure out the best ways to change themselves. Her audiences ended up carrying out diagnostic exercises, mostly centered on how to drive decision making lower in the organization and solve problems close to the customer, but it was a small part of the overall work they were able to complete even before the kickoff events were over. Needless to say, the events launched real corporate change on a grand level and led to many other changes, both big and small, that eased bureaucracy, saved money, and pushed authority further toward the front lines in the organization.

For advanced users: Involve your audience anywhere you can.

Now that you've got the idea about the action step, take these examples and categories back to the rest of the speech and see where else you can get the audience involved. Can you begin with a simple, nonthreatening form of play? I once had an IT expert begin a talk on how the Internet (and IT in general) was making it possible to wrap services around products by holding up tubes of toothpaste (purchased in the hotel store) and asking,

"Is this a product or a service?" To every comment she got, she responded, "Right!" and handed out the tube of toothpaste to the lucky winner. The point was that a tube of toothpaste could be both a product and a service with an embedded chip in it that would re-order the toothpaste when the tube got low. This opening enabled her to frame the discussion around how embedded chips could make it possible for dumb products in general to become smart services.

The result was a lot of laughter and goodwill generated at the beginning of the talk, which helped launch what was otherwise a fairly technical discussion of Internet business models.

But the other secret of that opening was even more fundamental: It brought the speaker into close contact with selected members of the audience and gave them a (modest) kinesthetic experience (of clutching a tube of toothpaste). Both those activities helped raise the kinesthetic energy in the room.

And here's the point: The research on learning says that we're all kinesthetic, visual, and auditory learners to some extent. Think about most business presentations. They have no kinesthetic stimulation, very little visual stimulation (unless you find the bewildering variety of PowerPoint fonts stimulating), and only a modest amount of auditory excitement (most speakers use a monotone).

By working audience participation exercises into your speeches, you can ensure that your audience members get some measure of greater interest through kinesthetic, visual, and auditory channels. You can get them to move around the room, draw pictures, talk to each other—anything that begins to address the need to escape the sensory deprivation chamber that is the modern business presentation, all white noise, low lighting, and voices that hum quietly in the distance. But more about this important work in part III, where we tackle rehearsal.

Remember

There are four good ways to involve your audience:

- **TEACH:** Get the audience to take what they've learned and test it against someone else, or coach someone else in their development.

- **TELL A STORY:** Get the audience to weave their personal stories into the larger one that the speaker has just told.

- **PLAY:** Get the audience to compete or play in some way to make the point of the talk real.

- **DESIGN:** Get the audience to design a path forward, or next steps, or complete a diagnostic exercise.

Use these categories to design action steps and for interaction with the audience throughout the presentation.

There are no rules here except one: *Whatever you get the audience to do must reinforce in some way your elevator speech.*

Martin Luther King, Jr., Shares an Unforgettable Dream

Martin Luther King, Jr., gave what is often called the greatest speech of the twentieth century on a sweltering day in August 1963 before a huge crowd spread across the Mall in Washington, D.C. What made the speech so great? A quick look at King's technique yields some insights that can improve your public presentations, too—even if your audience is less than half a million people and your venue less imposing than our nation's capital.

King made it conversational.

Many people have heard of the "I Have a Dream" speech. But few know that the speech (and the audience) really came alive about halfway through King's prepared text when, sensing that he was not reaching his audience as he wanted to, King actually began speaking extemporaneously. He put down the prepared speech, looked directly at the audience, and spoke from the heart. The result was electric. Studying the film of the speech shows that the audience began to respond shortly thereafter, shouting their approval of phrase after phrase, culminating in the unforgettable roar that greeted King's final lines: *"Free at last! Free at last! Thank God Almighty, we are free at last!"*

King made artful use of repetition.

Drawing on his background as a Baptist preacher, King structured the ad-libbed portion of his speech by stating a new thought and then elaborating on it. Next he would repeat the original phrase and elaborate some more. The resulting repetition helped both the speaker and the audience keep track of where he was. The open-ended nature of this structure allowed King to work a phrase until he had exhausted it and then move on, without confusing the audience.

I say to you today, my friends, that in spite of the difficulties and frustrations of the moment I still have a dream. It is a dream deeply rooted in the American dream. I have a dream that one day this nation will rise up and live out the true meaning of its creed: "We hold these truths to be self-evident; that all men are created equal." I have a dream that one day on the red hills of Georgia the sons of former slaves and the sons of former slave owners will be able to sit down together at the table of brotherhood. I have a dream that one day even the state of Mississippi, a desert state sweltering [in] the heat of injustice and oppression, will be trans-formed into an oasis of freedom and justice. I have a dream that my four little children will one day live in a nation where they will not be judged by the color of their skin but by the content of their character. I have a dream today.

Contrast this fluidity with the more formal opening of the speech, where King uses an extended metaphor—"a promissory note"—that is more compelling on paper than in presentation mode. "When the architects of our republic wrote the magnificent words of the Constitution and the Declaration of Independence, they were signing a promissory note to which every American was to fall heir."

King used familiar language known to every American.

As King warmed to his task, he quoted Biblical phrases and national songs well-known to his listeners. Then he elaborated upon those references and made them relevant to his theme of working toward racial equality and harmony. By referring to well-known material, he brought his audience along with him, allowing them better to grasp his theme when he connected that to the familiar lore: "This will be the day when all of God's children will be able to sing with new meaning 'My country 'tis of thee, sweet land of liberty, of thee I sing. Land where my fathers died, land of the pilgrim's pride, from every mountainside, let freedom ring.' And if America is to become a great nation this must become true."

King let his audience know exactly where he stood.

The most frequently missed opportunity in business presentations today is the presenter telling the audience how she feels about the topic. What do you care about? Why? What is important to you about the topic? Audiences very much want to know the answers to those questions, because they help the listeners know what's essential to take away from the talk. King left his audience in no doubt how he felt about his topic. Charisma comes from passion about the topic, appropriately expressed, and King excelled here.

This is our hope. This is the faith with which I return to the South. With this faith we will be able to hew out of the mountain of despair a stone of hope. With this faith we will be able to transform the jangling discords of our nation into a beautiful symphony of brotherhood. With this faith we will be able to work together, to pray together, to struggle together, to go to jail together, to stand up for freedom together, knowing that we will be free one day.

Even the FBI informants among the listeners were impressed with King's power and sincerity.

PART III

Rehearsing the Presentation

CHAPTER 10

Search for the Truth (*Rehearsing*)

RECENTLY, I WAS WORKING WITH A client—let's call him Josh—who had many years of experience in the consulting business. His assignment was to give a speech to more than five hundred clients and potential clients. It was a big deal; a biannual event that was a kind of marker for the firm, a measure of its current successes and its plans for the future. Josh had given many speeches in his twenty-five years of consulting, to audiences large and small. For all his experience, he didn't enjoy himself as much as he should, and he didn't connect with audiences as much as he might have, given his status and all he had to offer.

An interesting concept that ties
your physical comfort and expressiveness to
your presentation effectiveness
(part of your charisma)

Find the kinesthetic truth of a great presentation.

What was missing? His speech draft was unexceptional. It had been pulled together by Josh's research assistants and the team working on the event. It was full of solid business insights, all relevant to the theme of the conference.

Josh was certainly familiar with the material, and he had prepared for the rehearsal. But as he began to work through the draft, it became apparent that he was not connecting with the content in any real way. His body language gave him away; it was disengaged, lifeless, and uncomfortable.

I called a halt to the proceedings and asked Josh what was wrong. He wasn't sure. In fact, he wasn't really aware that anything was wrong. He always felt this way delivering a speech, he reported.

We turned to a videotape of an earlier presentation Josh had given to an audience of similar size. As we watched it, I saw Josh mirroring the uncomfortable body language of the tape. On the tape, Josh was working hard. He was trying to make up with energy and sheer volume what was lacking in his gut—any real sense that what he was saying really mattered.

Finally, I confronted him. "Josh, you don't believe this speech. What do you believe?"

After much discussion, Josh confessed that his years of experience in consulting had given him a nicely jaundiced view of the current buzzwords and business ideas. "I've seen it all before," Josh said, showing real passion for the first time that afternoon. "We were recommending the same approach a decade ago. There's nothing new under this particular sun. People should understand that they need to hold fast to a couple of time-tested truths and execute properly. It's not about following the latest fad."

We had found the speech that Josh needed to give. Once he connected with the wisdom that he had acquired during his years in the business and was able to express it, a number of interesting insights emerged, providing the basis of a successful speech.

What's more, Josh gave a speech that was wholly engaged for the first time in his career. He had the audience with him from the very start, and when he called me the next morning, he reported that he was still sailing on the adrenaline the experience had given him. He was the hit of the show.

That's why you need to rehearse.

There was nothing wrong with Josh's speech on paper. It was smart, sensible, and well-organized. But it was not a speech that Josh could give with any conviction.

A speech is never real until you give it. You can't experience it solely on paper—or PowerPoint.

And yet business speakers everywhere try this gambit over and over again. Perhaps they remember clearly the one time out of ten when they "winged it" and it went reasonably well. Lightning does have to strike somewhere, after all. But most speakers' memories are distressingly selective and give a highly colored view of the success of the presentation. Get an anonymous poll of the audience and see what effect the speech actually had.

Why skip rehearsal, in spite of overwhelming evidence that it's not a good idea? Most people are so nervous about public speaking that they'd rather put everything about it off as long as possible rather than confront their fears.

That's why so many presentations are so mediocre. The good news is that with a little forethought, preparation and—yes—rehearsal, you can deliver a presentation that connects with your audience intellectually, emotionally, and kinesthetically, and that moves them to action.

Let's say that I've convinced you, and you're never going to give another speech without rehearsing it beforehand. Just what am I talking about? How much work is involved, and what kind?

I'm going to suggest a whole series of ways to rehearse. Each one is designed to address a different speaking problem or issue.

You don't have to undertake them all; just the ones that will help you the most. But if you're not rehearsing at least three times before a significant speech, then you're not taking the event seriously enough for success. For lesser speeches to smaller groups, one rehearsal may be enough. It depends on your comfort level, familiarity with the group, and how well you know the material.

But at least always rehearse the essence and the opening story, both described below, and some form of the entire speech. Try to make sure that at least one of those later rehearsals is in the room itself close to the day of the speech.

Begin by rehearsing the essence of your speech.

How to begin? If you've prepared an elevator speech, you have a good idea of what the essence of your talk is. You know what the main point is that you want your audience to take away. If the audience gets that one point, your speech is a success. If the audience fails to get that one point, you've failed.

So begin by rehearsing the main spine of your speech, including the elevator version. You should be able to run through the high-level structure of a sixty- to ninety-minute speech in roughly five to seven minutes, shorn of all the detail. I have run these kinds of rehearsals many times with clients, and a consistent danger sign comes when the speaker's "summary" lasts thirty minutes. It's a good signal that the presenter doesn't have a clear grasp of the essence of the talk.

It's not that you'll necessarily ever give the essence speech, but that you need to be very clear about the heart of your purpose in front of the audience. If you're not clear about what's most important, what's less important, and what's least important, how can you expect your audience to be? Audiences expect you to know—and to tell them—what the high points of your presentation are, and to signal clearly what is merely supporting material.

There's nothing more discomfiting for an audience than a speaker who appears to be wandering in a forest of mental confusion with no path to guide him out. That's a prison sentence of indeterminate length with no prospect for parole, and it's appalling for an audience to contemplate.

The one place, by the way, where you may give something like the essence speech is to media, although for television you'll have to break it down into even smaller, twelve-second chunks.

Once you've got the essence of your talk down, the outline or logical structure, then you're ready for nuance.

Practice the opening story by itself.

If you've followed my advice and developed a wonderful, short, thematically appropriate story to begin the presentation, then you need to put a good deal of energy into getting that story absolutely right. The typical mistakes that speakers make telling these stories have to do with detail, language, and emotion.

Too much detail kills a good story.

The usual problem here is too much detail, of the irrelevant sort. Again, look at Jesus' parables in the New Testament as a guide. Those stories ruthlessly strip out all detail except the few key bits that give the story the credence and particularity it needs to bring it to life.

The moment you say, "Last Tuesday—or was it Wednesday—no, actually I think it was Friday because that's the day my husband picks up the dry cleaning and he was late . . . " you've first irritated and then lost your audience. It's amazing how quick audiences are to sense irrelevant detail. So you need to practice your story again and again, each time eliminating detail until you actually are stripping out meaning. The sad truth is that no one is as interested in your stories as you, unless you're a film star. Even then, you're only as good as your last picture, so don't push your luck!

Use language with precision.

Conversationally, most people fill their silences with apologetic language that friends are mostly willing to tolerate but that audiences will find tedious and deflating. Don't say, "As I entered that interview room, I reflected that I really, really wanted the job." Rather, say something like, "I entered the interview room desperately wanting the job." Or perhaps even better, "I went into the interview wanting the job."

So cut out extraneous adjectives, qualifiers, and other such weasel words. Do I need to tell you to avoid words and noises like *like, you know, uh,* and *sort of*? If your language is sprinkled with such abominations, pay someone to sit in the audience every time you speak and keep count. Then fine yourself a dollar for every such barbarism. As the dollar total mounts, you'll find yourself eschewing these words in favor of fiscal responsibility.

Find the emotion in the story.

Your emotional language and signals are important everywhere during a presentation, but especially so during the opening story. The best way to test this is to write out the story and mark the emotions you're trying to convey at each turn of the tale. If you don't know what they are, that's a sign that the story needs more work!

Then tell the story to a small group and ask them to identify the emotions they're seeing. If they're not seeing the ones you think you're emoting, you need to get to work. If they're not seeing any emotions, you need to work on that, too. Practice exaggerating the emotional content until you find the right balance between hysteria and clarity.

Practice the big emotional stretch.

Which brings me to another very valuable kind of rehearsal—the big emotional stretch.

Is this with drwg?

One of the results of adrenaline in the body, the sort of adrenaline that comes about from having to give a speech, is that you shut down all your systems except the most basic ones that support life. You keep breathing, just, but most of the rest of it goes away. Of course, the extent of this phenomenon depends on just how much adrenaline you have coursing through your system, but it doesn't take much before the natural qualities of your speech start to erode.

You become a lifeless automaton, speaking to the audience in a flat, expressionless voice, frozen in one spot like the proverbial possum in the headlights.

To fight against that, you need to develop the muscles used in expressing a variety of emotions even though you're terrified.

Here's how you do it. Pick a very simple emotional spectrum, such as happy to sad. Then give some piece of your speech to a small audience of pets and children. When they shout out, "Happy!" you give the next few sentences in the speech as if you were the happiest person on the planet. (Think Captain Kirk meeting a new female life form. First chew the scenery. Then the female.) They let you run for thirty seconds or so, shouting at you to get happier and happier. The point is, it's never enough. Make it bigger! Not big enough! You can do more! Come on! You're looking a little happier now—go for broke! *Get happy!*

Then your audience will shout "Sad!" and you will give the next section of your speech as if you were sadder than Attorney General John Ashcroft talking about homeland security. Much sadder. Cry if you can, but get *real sad*.

Actors find these emotions by thinking of really happy or sad things that have happened to them and using the emotional memory to link to the words in the moment they're experiencing now. It works, but it takes a lot of practice. All you're looking for in this rehearsal is to get comfortable with bigger feelings, facial expressions, gestures, and motions than you are now. You don't need precision here. You're not going for an Academy Award. And the point is not to be appropriate in this rehearsal

to the actual text or meaning of your speech. In part, by decou-
pling the emotion from the meaning in the text, you can get the
cartoonish excess we're looking for here. We want overacting,
because we know that in the real event, you'll pull back.

Try babbling to increase your nonverbal power.

A related genre of rehearsal to the emotional swings exercise is
the Babbling Rehearsal. For this one, take your essence speech
and give it not with words but with nonsense phrases, gestures,
and body language. The point is that you're not allowed to say
meaningful words, but you are to *think* them. You're going to try
to get as much across as possible. It's not charades, but it is the
next thing to it. Use your hands, your body, your face, to get as
much of the meaning across as possible. Short of sign language,
everything is permissible. You are to approach this exercise as if
it really were possible to give the essence of your speech in five
minutes using babble words and have the audience understand
what you said.

Some clients find this exercise hideously difficult, because they
are unable to utter meaningless sounds without lots of practice.
For the truly babble-challenged, I recommend using several
sounds that you work out in advance over and over again, rather
than trying to be spontaneous about it. Lewis Carroll is a good
source of excellent nonsense words—try "brillig, slithy, toves,
wabe, mimsy, borogroves, mome, outgrabe" on for size. Does that
help? You could even just say, "Blah, blah, blah," but that gets
very monotonous very quickly.

So you stand there, feeling foolish, in front of that small audience you've carefully selected. You've got the essence speech written out on cards, or at least in note form. As you begin, saying
something like, "Mishnoony tabo romepuyshkin barangy," you
are thinking the exact equivalent in real words. And you gesture,

grimace, emote, and move your body in any way you can think of to get your meaning across.

It won't work very well. You won't get much across. But <u>you will expand your expressive range greatly, and that is the point of the exercise.</u> Hint: Once again, emotions play a big part here. If you are clear about what your emotional attitude toward your material is, it will be much easier to get at least some meaning across. Most of our decoding of emotional meaning comes not from content but from gesture and tone of voice.

Once you've finished, ask the audience what they got out of your amazing performance. If someone says something like, "Well, I didn't get much, but I could tell that there was something in a box and you really hated that, and you wanted to get that thing out of the box," that would be a raving success.

Try using another persona.

This form of rehearsal is a variant on the other attempts to get you to be more comfortable expressing emotional meaning along with the content. For some people, expression as themselves is difficult, but when they take on the role of a favorite character, or movie star, or politician—whoever gets their juices flowing—then something releases inside them and they permit themselves to become much more expressive.

Is it Humphrey Bogart that floats your boat? Or Golda Meir? Or Winston Churchill? Or Margaret Thatcher? Pick someone that you really idolize or have watched a hundred times, or that friends tell you looks just like you, or you do a great imitation of —whatever the connection, pick a hero. Then give the speech as if that hero were giving it. Imitate style, mannerisms, voice, gesture, content, everything you can think of. If you're giving a presentation about launching a new product, how would Bogart have done it? Would he have said, "I think this is the beginning of a beautiful friendship between the consumer and Incredible Edible Munchies?"

Does that make your skin crawl? Good, it's supposed to. This is not about art, it's about finding ways to free yourself to become more emotionally expressive. Period. All the great works of the cinema and the great speeches of all the politicians of the last several thousand years are at your disposal here. Just imitate someone who engages you imaginatively and emotionally.

By the way, it can be John Wayne or Clint Eastwood, but those aren't the best possible choices. Tough guys who hold everything back are not the best models for public speakers. In fact, too much—and too slavish—imitation of John Wayne is partly responsible for many of the poor business speakers out there of a certain generation. It is interesting in the close-up format of film when an actor holds something back, but not from fifty feet away. It simply looks like the actor (or speaker) isn't doing much of anything.

Learn from the master: Watch the "I Have a Dream" speech.

For your final variety of piecemeal rehearsal before we get to the whole speech, try giving the end of your presentation as if it were a political stump speech, finishing with all the passion at your command. You're trying to get out the vote, or motivate people to change society, or at least remember your name. The beginnings and endings of presentations are the parts that audiences remember, so you need to work on both. Give that ending as if your life depended on it. Shout it out! Don't hold back. For inspiration, take a look at video clips of the end of Martin Luther King, Jr.'s famous "I Have a Dream" speech. He works up to a fabulous crescendo, as only someone schooled in the language and rhythms of Baptist preaching can. When he finally shouts,

"Free at last, free at last, thank God Almighty, we are free at last!" it takes a hard heart indeed to remain indifferent.

That's what you're striving for here. Shout it like you mean it, or at least like King meant it.

In chapter 11, we'll rehearse the whole speech, at least three times.

Remember

There are a variety of ways to focus on rehearsing a speech and parts of a speech. Use the ones that seem most useful to you.

- **ESSENCE**—the outline or spine of the speech

- **THE OPENING STORY**

- **BIG EMOTIONAL STRETCH**—giving parts of the speech with huge emotion

- **BABBLING**—using nonsense words to concentrate on the nonverbal

- **ANOTHER PERSONA**—to help you transcend your own limitations

- **I HAVE A DREAM**—the political stump speech as a model

CHAPTER 11

Choreograph
the Kinesthetics

✳✳

NOW WE'RE GOING TO REHEARSE THE whole thing, at least three times. This is nonnegotiable for big speeches, and recommended (depending on your level of experience) for lesser speeches where the stakes are still high. Actors preparing a stage show typically rehearse daily for six *weeks* before opening night. You need at least three tries. The point is that you need to get some familiarity with the material, the length of it, as well as the meaning, so that you're not shocked by it the first time in front of a live "real" audience. You can pick and choose among the rehearsal formats in the previous chapter depending on your needs and concerns. But you should at least do the following when the stakes are high: Rehearse the whole talk once for kinesthetics, once for transitions, and once putting it all together.

Rehearse for the kinesthetics.

Now it's time to get the choreography right. And this is the single most important thing to get right after the content. If you've got good content you're passionate about and you've got the kinesthetics down, you will give a memorable speech.

The research on the space between people reveals four distinct zones. Within each, behavior and relationship is different. You, as a speaker, need to match the space with the desired behavior and relationship. It's that simple—and that tricky.

Twelve feet or more is public space. From twelve feet to four feet is social space. From four feet to a foot and a half is personal space. And, in most Western cultures, less than a foot and a half is intimate space.

Public speaking since the ancient Greeks had been a matter of public space—large outdoor gatherings—and the large gestures and voice necessary to reach the audience in that kind of (unamplified) space. A look at rhetoric manuals from as recently as the nineteenth and early twentieth centuries will reveal instructions on the sweeping gestures that convey emotions and meaning, like astonishment, fear, happiness, and sorrow. In addition, much discussion of sound projection and voice production follows, because you couldn't be heard in large outdoor spaces without microphones unless you knew how to breathe, to create sound, and to throw it to the farthest spectators.

All of that changed with the advent of amplification, radio, and television. First, people by and large forgot the art of projection, with the exception of some classically trained stage actors. Second, gesture got smaller and smaller as the movies and television brought us close to our public figures.

Public speaking today takes place in personal space.

Third, and most important, our whole idea of what constitutes a relationship with those public figures changed. Think about what a television picture does to someone like a newscaster or a guest on a talk show. When the camera is giving us a tight shot just on one figure, we usually get head and shoulders, and perhaps the top of a desk. The effect is to bring that person close to us, *as if they were about four feet away, or in our personal space.*

This is incredibly important to grasp, because it has changed the whole nature of the public discourse since Kennedy and Nixon debated on television in 1960. Think about it. We respond personally to these figures now, because in our minds we have had them in our personal space. This phenomenon accounts for that bizarre sense even sophisticated people have that they "know" or "own" their public figures.

It's personal now. That's our expectation. And yet, think about most business presentations. The speaker hides behind a podium, rarely moving out toward the audience, and drones on for an hour or ninety minutes about a subject few people in the room feel connected to.

Contrast that with, say, David Letterman, who's in our personal space, speaks in short bursts, and laughs a lot, all the while sharing that personal space of ours with the most interesting public figures of the day. Is it any wonder we like Letterman and despise the vice president of marketing?

More than that, while Letterman is conversational and casual in his speech, the business speaker still clings to the clumsy phrasing and stuffy sense that he should tell the audience what he's going to say, say it, and then repeat, telling the audience what he said.

Boring. Impersonal. Not intimate. Not interesting. Not at all like Letterman.

So it's time to put an end to all that. Here's what you can do: Give a conversational, interesting speech you're passionate about, moving into the personal space of selected members of the audience as you reach the points in your speech that need to be emphasized the most, or are the most personal, or are the key takeaways.

That's what I mean by choreography.

Find the key points of the talk and move toward your audience while delivering them.

Here's how you rehearse it. You're going to begin the speech with that amazing little parable you've worked up, right? OK. What I want you to do (we're in rehearsal mode here, pretending there's an audience of the size you will actually face) is to make eye contact with someone in the front right quadrant of the audience and move toward them as you're telling the story. When you get to the most important line, I want you to be four feet or less (but not closer than a foot and a half) from that person. Finish telling the story to that individual and then move back to your central spot, where your notes or your computer or the overhead projector is.

Then, begin the next section of the speech—the problem statement—with someone in the left rear quadrant of the audience in your sights. Move toward that person as you make your next point. Don't endanger yourself or the audience trying to get close to that person. Merely get as close as the seating allows. If you end up still quite a distance away, make good eye contact, finish your point, and then move back to parade rest.

Get the idea? You should grab a bit of your talk, find an audience member, move toward that person, deliver the point, and then move away. You don't want to be rushing around like a hyperkinetic madman, but you don't want to move too slowly either. Think in terms of one to three minutes per point and per person, and vary the duration of your points so that it doesn't get too predictable or boring.

The idea is to get a thought, an idea, take it to an audience member, deliver it, pause to make sure that the proxy member of the audience has gotten the point, and then go back and get another one. A point can be up to five minutes long in a ninety-minute speech, but no longer. People will wonder why you're spending so much time with one person in the audience. If the person is an attractive member of the opposite sex, they won't wonder, they'll suspect. Neither outcome is preferable, so don't do it. Give everyone some time.

Divide the audience into convenient quadrants.

With audiences of roughly fifty people or more, divide the audience up into the four quadrants of front left and right, and back left and right. If you've got a smaller audience, fine. Make it simpler. If you've got twenty or fewer, and you're speaking for an hour or more, there's no reason why you can't get into the personal space of everyone there.

Don't confuse personal space with intimate space. Never crowd into an audience member's intimate space. It's the public speaking equivalent of rape. Don't do it.

I do it for effect when I'm giving talks on public speaking, but I set up the point elaborately beforehand and warn the victim, and we all have a good laugh. The typical reaction, incidentally, is for the victim to rear back with his or her head, graphically illustrating better than I could preach just how invasive that feeling is.

To be sure, different cultures have different boundaries to these four zones. Some Asian and Mediterranean cultures, for example, have a tighter sense of intimate space than eighteen inches, but every culture has the four zones. That means you can manipulate the sense of personal contact and public discourse wherever you speak to strengthen the bond with your audience. It just helps to know the local norms.

The key is, basically, to move toward your audience when you're saying something important, and to move away from them when you're finished, you're in transition, or you're going to cue up the next slide. At key moments in your talk, you want to be in the personal space (within four feet, but no closer than eighteen inches) to a selected proxy in your audience. At less important times, social space will do. Just indicate by your eye contact and body positioning that you're including more than one person at a time.

Avoid the PowerPoint trap.

Don't make the classic mistake many a PowerPoint jockey makes when you're finishing your comments on one particular slide. Since the mind usually moves faster than the tongue, your jockey will start moving toward the computer to cue up the next slide while still talking about the last. The effect is to confuse the audience. On the one hand, it's trying to understand the closing point on the slide, presumably an important one. On the other hand, the speaker is demonstrating with his body that what he's saying is not important, because he's moving away. It simply doesn't work. Body language and content are at war (unless you often say unimportant things). Instead, finish the point with feet firmly planted facing the audience, *then* pause for a second, and *only then* begin to move toward the computer and the next slide.

Good advice

If you are an inveterate PowerPoint user, you will also want to avoid the Circle of Death School of Speaker Choreography, where the presenter moves from peering at the screen while gesturing vaguely at some point on it, then moving back to the computer or overhead projector to cue up the next slide, to standing in front of the screen, squinting out at a vaguely outlined audience made virtually invisible by the bright light of the projector.

Ironically, presenters who move in this way usually finish their speeches thinking they are long-suffering heroes because they toughed out the bright lights and kept trying to look for their audience despite the difficulties. But who asked them to position themselves where they did? Why didn't they simply make their movements toward the audience when they had a point to make, and away, back to the computer, when it was time to change?

Even better, don't move toward the computer at all. Get a remote infrared clicker and stay focused on the audience at all times (better). Or do away with the slides altogether (best). You ask, how can you gesture toward the screen? My response is, why do you need to? If your slides are so complicated that you really need to walk the audience through them, they're much too complicated for a good presentation. Simplify them. A slide should be instantly understandable, or at least graspable, without elaborate explanation. Period.

Is this beginning to make sense to you? The point is that you are competing in the public discourse with television figures. That point is so important that I'll say it again: You are competing in the mind of your audience with television personalities. Television has created in us a need for personal connection with our public figures. You need to fulfill that expectation by connecting personally with your audience at meaningful places during your talk. If you do, you will not only increase your audience's understanding of your presentation, but also its sense of connection with you.

Fortunately, one of the characteristics of an audience is that it acts like a single mind. If you make eye contact with one person in the second row, right side, then everyone over there will feel more connected to you. If you cover the audience by quadrant, you will bring them all in, through individual proxies in each area. You can, by the way, cover several sides of the audience at once by moving toward, say, the left front, while at the same time making eye contact with the back right. But this move is for experienced presenters only; it takes presence of mind to accomplish it convincingly and without bumping into the furniture.

Rehearse the transitions.

One of the easiest ways for me to spot an underprepared presentation, especially one using PowerPoint, is the transitions. Someone who has thought enough about the whole speech will have a good sense of the overall story. There will be a clear sense of direction, hierarchy, and shape to the talk. On the other hand, a presentation that has been put together by the team at the last minute as a collection of slides will be like a collection of railroad cars—on the same track, but with no necessary connection beyond the fact that one comes after another.

You can always tell, because the speaker will eventually lapse into language like this: "[*Cues next slide.*] OK, what this slide shows is that blah blah blah. [*Cues next slide.*] OK, what this slide is showing is that blah blah blah."

There's a kind of monotony that sets in, a universal signal to the audience that what it is hearing is the lowest-common-denominator business presentation: a boring data dump pulled together quickly and looked at for the first time by both speaker and audience right then. Transitions may be, in fact, the single most important reason that so many business presentations that use PowerPoint are so bad.

So instead of falling into that trap, rehearse the speech with the sole purpose of finding what the connections are between the slides, or the items on the outline, or the main points of your essence speech. Go back over these moments until you have each one right, so that it is not simple for an audience member to tell when you're moving from one slide or topic to another.

If you're stuck, by the way, on a transition, and can't come up with some convincing way to get from A to B, then the logic of the talk may be at fault. Or you may simply need to jump from A to B without apology. Sometimes the best transition is none at all. In most cases, simple is better than elaborate.

Have a dress rehearsal.

Here's where you finally put it all together. This rehearsal needs to be in the real room where you're going to present, by the way, with the real lighting, stage, props, screens—whatever will go into making the experience, short of the real audience.

The closer to the real thing, the better. I have noticed that speakers can handle the first curve thrown at them on the day of the presentation. They can handle the second. And most can handle a third. But after that, they start to come unglued. If the lights aren't quite what you expected, you squint and survive. Add to that a problem with the projector, and you're stressed but hanging in there. On top of that, put in a larger-than-expected audience, and you're still fighting. But now throw in a hostile question in the first five minutes, and you're in for trouble. I've seen the results too many times, and they're not pretty.

But you're smarter than that; you've insisted on a full rehearsal in the space. And it's the day before, not the midnight before, so you're reasonably alert and you have time to make small changes to the talk or the setting if necessary. Sometimes, of course, it's impossible to get into the space beforehand. Sometimes you can only get in for a quick look. Do the best you can and use whatever opportunity you can get. The more you're used to the space, the less energy you'll have to put in focusing on it and the more you can put on the audience.

Here's what I want you to do first, assuming you do get to rehearse on the spot. Go to the front of the room, where you'll begin your talk. Look around. Take in the entire space. Now, walk all the way around it. Get your body all over that room. Look at the stage, or the place you'll be speaking from, from every possible position an audience member will occupy. Stand in the doorway and imagine yourself as a latecomer, checking out the scene, trying to decide whether or not to sit down. Look at the lighting from various angles.

The "Walk Around"

The point is to learn viscerally how big the room is and what it looks like from the audience's point of view. This simple exercise will help you connect with them and project to them. A classic mistake most speakers make is to talk to the front few rows of listeners, all but forgetting the folks in the back.

Now find a slightly deaf friend, position him as far from you as possible, and practice speaking to that distant, deaf person so that he has no difficulty understanding you, using the first few lines of the speech. Never forget him. If you start talking to the front rows, again, think of him. He's in the room, too, and he wants to be included. He can't be if he can't hear you.

Next, it's time to get comfortable in the space. Stand, arms at your sides, feet shoulder-width apart, facing the imaginary audience. Now tense and relax individual sets of muscles, beginning with your feet and working all the way up to your face. Grab the floor as if you were an eagle with talons, grasping right through your shoes into the floor. Squeeze tightly. Then relax. Repeat, for all the muscle groups, including the embarrassing ones, all the way up to your scalp.

Then, give yourself a very gentle facial massage with your hands. Gently rub your forehead, your eyes (very gently), your cheeks, and especially your jawline from ear to chin. Waggle your jaw by dropping it down, loosely, as if you were really amazed at how much fun this is, and grasp under your lip and chin with your right hand. Gently wiggle your jaw up and down. Let go. Stick your tongue out and move it around as if you were Mick Jagger trying to sing "Angie" by drawing out the "A" sound for the entire song. Drop your head to your chest, and let it hang. Make the same Jaggeresque sounds again, sticking out your tongue. Finally, roll your shoulders forward and back.

Do you notice places of tension? Everyone has them; some people get tense in their lower back, others in their shoulders, and many people in the muscles of their face. Wherever you find tension, work especially on those areas to release it and to relax. Remember those areas of special tension so that you can give them some good exercise on the morning of the event.

Feel better? Good. By now, you should have a good sense of the room, what it looks like from the audience's point of view, and how hard you have to work to fill it, as well as how far you need to move to make contact with everyone in the audience, at least through the relevant proxies in each quadrant. You should have a good sense of where you tend to gather muscular tension under conditions of adrenaline, and you should have made some effort to relax those areas. So you're present in the room, you're relaxed, you're focused on the speech, and you're ready to go.

Give the talk. All the way through. No interruptions. Just like you were doing it for an audience. If you've got a small audience of colleagues, other speakers, audiovisual people, great. You need to pretend that there's an audience there, of the actual size and shape of the real one, so that you can practice your choreography on them. This is when you find out if you can walk and talk at the same time. In the dress rehearsal, you'll find out whether or not you've got all the transitions down, and you'll discover the kind of stamina that it takes you to get through the talk. You'll try out your movements toward the audience. And you'll get an idea of how long the talk will take, always understanding that every-thing takes longer when there's a real audience to contend with, even though it feels shorter to you.

If you do have a small audience, ask them not to give you feed-back until you're done. You want to get a sense of the rhythm of what you're doing now, and interruptions are not helpful for that. If they do give you feedback, ideally it should not be about the content of the talk at this stage, but only about delivery. Of course, if your boss is in the room watching and wants you to change the talk, that's life. But otherwise try to avoid it. New lines for opening night is every actor's nightmare, and there's good reason for that. It adds another unknown to a high-stress situation that already has too many. The point is to control variables, not increase their number.

In chapter 12, we'll put the focus back where it belongs, on the audience.

Remember

- Rehearse important speeches for the kinesthetics and transitions, and do at least one dress rehearsal where you put it all together.

- Use the four zones of space to underline the meaning of your speech and connect with the audience.

- Move toward your audience when you're making an important point.

- Practice making smooth transitions between your topics—or your slides, if you use them.

- Try to rehearse at least once in the space itself so that you get used to it.

CHAPTER 12

Pay Attention to What
Your Audience Needs

WELL, YOU'VE RESOLVED TO rehearse at least three times, and you've agreed to try to stretch yourself in a few areas where you think you may be weak. You're not done. It's time to put the emphasis back on the audience— yes, even during the rehearsal process.

This step is not about fundamentally changing the content of your talk. It's about further shaping, cutting, and trimming what's already there, on your feet with the audience in mind. If there are gaps to be filled, or parts that need to be cut, they are best discovered in rehearsal.

To understand where we're headed next, you have to recall what you know about learning styles. Many people are familiar with the three learning styles, typically referred to as the visual, auditory, and kinesthetic. Fewer have connected those with the crucial *levels* of learning that we all need to employ before we can truly know something—the intellectual, the emotional, and the physical. And fewer still apply these regularly to presentations. Is it any wonder, then, that most business presentations are only half-engaging and are quickly forgotten?

Let's say that you've created your speech according to the process I've outlined in part II. You've thought a lot about what the audience wants and how it thinks. You've worked on a few ways to get the audience involved, certainly at the end, but also, let's hope, throughout the speech. As you're working your way through the rehearsal process, getting a feel for the rhythms of the speech and its choreography, try to imagine an audience present. Look hard for the places in the speech that begin to feel long. Are there moments when you feel the need for a change of pace? Attention spans last about twenty minutes, so at minimum you need something in the way of a shift in the talk at least that often. But you also need to think about the different needs of those individuals in the audience.

Use PowerPoint for visual learners as if it were arsenic—carefully and in small doses.

You're probably a PowerPoint user, and you think that you've appealed to the visual learner because you've used slides. But the usual business slide is covered with words, and what visual learners need is pictures. What's more, they learn best from simple pictures. So connect your key concepts visually to triangles, circles, squares, and the like. Don't get fancy. It's simply not necessary, and it doesn't promote learning. In addition to pictures, you can use graphic illustrations, tables and charts, video, and the like for variety, but keep in mind that simpler is usually better.

For example, pie charts are good slide material; tables that have the same information expressed as numbers are not. As you're rehearsing, then, keep looking for ways to simplify those slides. Ask your colleagues and friends to suggest ideas.

Here's the way to think about visuals, especially PowerPoint. It's the way that writers of Broadway musicals think about the songs. They put in a song when the emotion of the moment demands something more than words. That's why the stars are always breaking into song when they realize that they love each other, for example. You should use PowerPoint just as sparingly. Don't think of it as wallpaper that's always there behind you, but a discrete moment in your talk when you turn to an illustration because it's too difficult to put the idea into mere words.

If you apply this stringent test to your use of PowerPoint, you'll find that you use it much more sparingly and effectively.

When you do use PowerPoint or one of its rivals, a few simple rules can help avoid the usual mistakes. I actually like title slides that go up before you speak—at conferences where there will be a series of speakers, for example. It helps the audience keep track of what's coming up. But I don't like PowerPoint wallpaper while you're speaking. It's distracting for the audience and raises the awful risk that the audience will find it more interesting than you. Why test the concept?

So use PowerPoint for illustrations. Pictures. Graphs. Pie charts. That sort of thing. If you must use it for words, keep the words to a title, a couple of key bulleted concepts, and at most a "kicker"— a statement of implication at the bottom. No more than four bullets, and the bullets should never exceed a line. Otherwise they're not bullets, they're poorly worded sentences, and a tip-off that you're indulging in a speaker outline again.

Make your headline a complete sentence. Here's why. Rather than saying "Implications of Cost-Cutting on the Department," or some such, a full sentence will force you to say something like "Cost-cutting will mean the elimination of needed services." Do you see how the second statement is more interesting than the first? It tells you the thought, whereas the first headline just tells you that a thought is coming.

PowerPoint users have at their disposal a plethora of fonts, clip art, and bells and whistles that let items zoom in from the left or right or other such glittery effects. Eschew them. They are merely an apology for real thought. Stick to a full-sentence headline, a few bullets, and perhaps a kicker, if you must use words. Better: just a few pictures. Best: no slides at all.

Remember, a presentation is an act of persuasion. You're most persuasive when it's just you. If you ever ask someone to marry you, will you use slides?

Appeal to auditory learners through Story, but think about getting them active.

How do you reach auditory learners? Through talk. But certain kinds of talk work better than others. Storytelling is probably the best approach, and you've got at least one good story in your talk. Parables and anecdotes will appeal to this kind of learner and get stored most directly into the memory. In addition, you can employ discussion groups, debates, question-and-answer sessions, and the like—anything that gets people talking in ways that are more connected to Story than the usual discursive style of business speeches. As you rehearse, then, look for places where you can pause the flow of your brilliant rhetoric and invite the audience in.

The only way to appeal to kinesthetic learners is through activity.

And what about the kinesthetic learners? The key here is to get them doing something, practicing what you're preaching. Get them involved early and often through role playing, games, working with models, even creating charts and physical representations of what you want them to learn. Once again, you can begin to look for these moments during rehearsal, once you've got the intellectual content of the talk down.

The research shows that some 30 percent to 40 percent of the audience are visual learners, some 20 percent to 30 percent are auditory learners, and some 30 percent to 50 percent are kinesthetic learners. It is this last group that is most often neglected in business presentations. So much of the business world appeals to the head, not the body, and presentations are rarely exceptions to this dismal rule. You can increase your listeners' energy enormously at the opening of a speech by simply having them stand up and shout something appropriate or fun. It's corny, but it works.

Businesspeople like to be active. They are also adults. Let them do as much of the work of the presentation as possible, and they'll take it to heart more thoroughly. As you rehearse, look for places to relinquish control of the immediate agenda and let the audience take over the learning. It feels risky until you've done it a few times and discovered what a wonderful, energetic response you get from the audience. Then you'll never go back.

Remember

- In rehearsal, think about your audience and the three kinds of learners—visual, auditory, and kinesthetic.
- Appeal to all three kinds by understanding their needs and shaping aspects of your delivery accordingly.
- "Visuals" like simple pictures.
- "Auditories" like stories.
- "Kinesthetics" like movement.

CHAPTER 13

Conquer Your Fear

S O HOW DO YOU FEEL? ARE YOU
starting to get edgy? If you're a little nervous, that's good. You need the adrenaline
that's causing that sensation to give you the energy and charisma
to give a good speech. If you're terrified, that's not so good. It
may be time to address a few remarks not only to the nervous,
which is just about everybody, but also to the very, very nervous—a much smaller category.

I once sat on the red-eye from Los Angeles back to New York
with a gentleman—Chuck—who asked me what I did. When I
explained that I was a speech coach, he immediately started
twitching in his seat. Literally twitching—hands and feet going
in all directions, as if he had developed a sudden, inexplicable
whole-body itch. His reaction was extraordinary, and he was in
such evident distress that I had to ask him what was the matter.

"You don't understand," he said. "I've arranged my whole life so that I don't have to give speeches."

As we talked, it turned out that this person had actually risen to the level of senior vice president of a high-tech company *without ever giving a presentation of any kind*. I was so fascinated by the sheer difficulty of pulling this feat off that I asked him in some detail how he had managed.

The story he told was staggering. He had put an enormous amount of energy into evasion, lying, last-minute excuses, even travel—all to avoid giving talks, even routine briefings to his direct reports. A couple of his assistants were in on the secret, and they were used to standing in for him at the last moment, when he had suddenly taken sick, or discovered a soccer game he couldn't miss. He told me that virtually his entire extended family had died at least once in service to his phobia, so he could attend their funerals instead of giving talks. And most of that extended family was invented! He had to keep extensive notes on all the excuses he had used so that he could vary them appropriately and not fall prey to any obvious lies. It was sad to think what this man might have accomplished had he been able to put all this energy and invention into something productive—or even into fixing his little problem.

By the time he was finished with his confession to me, he was close to tears. He asked me if I could help him. I told him that I could, if he was ready to make the effort. He said that he was. We arranged an appointment for the following week on the East Coast.

The night before that appointment, I got a call from one of the Chuck's administrators. "Chuck is sorry," he said, "but he's got an emergency meeting that's come up and can't meet with you. Can we reschedule for next week?"

This tactic was repeated more than half a dozen times, each time with the reason escalated, until I got a call—once again the night before we were due to meet, this time in Boston—from Chuck himself.

"Nick," he said. "I'm at the airport."

"OK, so you're here; that's great. What's up?" I had a sense that all was not right.

"No, I mean the Los Angeles airport. LAX," Chuck said.

"What the hell are you doing there?" I was tired of all the evasions, and getting a bit short with him.

"Nick, I flew to Los Angeles to avoid meeting with you."

And that was that. That's speech phobia. If you're like Chuck, then you need a special program. In brief, what seems to work is some variant of desensitizing, a form of psychological conditioning. You begin by talking to an inanimate object, and gradually work up to a live human, and finally an audience. It's difficult, but it's quite achievable. It only takes putting in the time. There are coaches and psychologists who specialize in helping people get past speech phobia.

If you don't have speech phobia, then you're like most people. You've got some nervousness, and it varies depending on the occasion, the size of the audience, how prepared you are, and the like. Following are a few tips for you to minimize the agony.

First of all, do your homework.

One common source of speech anxiety is the fear that you will be caught out not knowing an answer, or shown up by someone in the audience who knows more than you. Your work on reducing fear thus should begin long before the actual speech. You can increase your comfort by thoroughly researching the topic, planning out what you want to say, and rehearsing. And rehearsing in different ways, in order to get at whatever is the particular cause of your nervousness.

Many speakers try to "wing" their remarks, and suffer accordingly. Their performances are uneven and depend on good fortune during the event itself. Why put yourself into harm's way? Why not know your topic and prepare well in advance of the event?

Try writing out the speech in its entirety before your rehearsal.

A standard fear that many people have is that they'll forget where they are at some point during the speech and go blank. The way to think about notes for your presentations is to have them in sufficient detail so that fear doesn't slow you down. If that means writing out the entire speech, then write out the entire speech. You will lose spontaneity in the delivery, but you won't be afraid. As time goes on, try reducing the amount of support you give yourself, until you're just using basic notes and can be appropriately conversational. If, when the day approaches, you're still quite dependent on a full or nearly full text, so be it. Better that you're a little stilted than so frightened that it all passes in a blur and you can't remember what you said. There's little hope of improving when you can't remember what you've done.

Visualize yourself being successful.

This technique will not work with the truly terrified, because they will be much too nervous to remember to visualize anything except themselves failing spectacularly. For the rest, good visualization can make the difference between average and excellent speech delivery. It takes real discipline to accomplish, however, because it must be practiced regularly beginning weeks or months before the event. The way visualization works is this: Whenever you find yourself thinking about the event, create a scenario *to which you return again and again* of yourself succeeding brilliantly. Make it as specific as possible. Visit the site well in advance of the day of the speech. Find out as much as you can about the event—the time of day, the setup of the room, the number of people involved, who they are, whether they will have just eaten or be expecting lunch, and so on—and use all that information to create a vivid series of mental images in which you arrive at the venue, enter the hall to wild acclaim, take the stage, wow the audience, and finish to a standing ovation. Afterward, you find yourself besieged on all sides by well-wishers, people handing you their business cards, and those who would simply touch the hem of your garments. The point is that every time your presentation creeps into your consciousness, you must go through this scenario. As you practice it, it will gradually crowd out the negative thoughts that can lead you on a downward spiral to debilitating nervousness on the day of the event itself.

As you rehearse, then, use the visualization you've created to begin your session. Any time you find yourself getting nervous, stop and revisualize. Then begin again. You need to emphasize the visualization during rehearsal, because when the performance comes, it's too late. You can't spend several minutes picturing yourself succeeding with the audience staring at you wondering if you've had some sort of stroke.

For the truly nervous, don't visualize: Begin by breathing.

It all begins with breathing. Belly breathing. If you're frightened, you tend to take shallow breaths. Unfortunately, shallow breaths are also a sign of fear for many of us. Hence, we create a vicious circle leading to ever-increasing terror, and all because we have to breathe to live. Moreover, most of us breathe incorrectly, sucking in with our stomachs and raising our shoulders when taking in air, and reversing the process when expelling air. The opposite is the correct way. You must use your diaphragmatic muscles, the ones that support your chest, to expand your lungs when you breathe in, and contract these muscles, shrinking your stomach, when you breathe out.

Practice your presence.

For years actors have developed their command of their bodies on stage—so-called stage presence—by focusing on exercises that bring them into the moment of being on stage in front of the audience, avoiding distracting thoughts of the past or the future. To develop your own presence, try this simple routine. Sit in a chair, with your hands on your knees, and say to yourself, "I am sitting in a chair with my hands on my knees." Between each word, lift your hands a few inches off your knees and then lower them after the next word. The effect will be to slow you down to an extent that will astonish you and make you feel ridiculous (it is important to practice this exercise in the privacy of your own home).

Once you have repeated this exercise many times, practice standing up and walking across the room to a predetermined point. Again, describe what you are doing as you take each step, word by word. Once you have mastered that, practice walking, talking, and carrying an object. The point of all this focus on apparently simple tasks is that you will eventually be able to carry that intense focus in front of an audience. The secret is that when you are focused on your own actions (and not, it is important to realize, on your fears) the audience will be, too. They won't be able to take their eyes off you.

Master the pause.

Many nervous speakers betray their nervousness by rushing off at a verbal gallop from the moment they are introduced to the audience. They never pause for breath until they are done. This deplorable activity has the unfortunate result of making it so much harder for your audiences to take in what you are saying that eventually they give up and tune out. As soon as you pick up on their inattentiveness, you begin to self-destruct, and the vicious cycle is complete.

Instead, just before you begin, pause until the audience is silent and attentive. You might even breathe here. Then begin, confidently and with focus.

In rehearsal, you can begin by sitting down in a chair at the front of the room and going through your exercise to reach the podium, or the spot where you will talk. Even that little bit of presence work will improve your charisma.

For the terror-stricken, don't make eye contact.

For those who are only temporarily terrified, steady eye contact of a few seconds' duration with selected individuals in the audience is still good advice. Don't scan rapidly or dart your eyes around the room; you'll look like a criminal who wants only to escape. But for those who are speech-phobic, no eye contact at all may be better. Until you become comfortable with the whole speech process, it may help to pretend the audience isn't there, just so that you can get through your talk.

In rehearsal, then, look up in the middle distance, over the heads of the audience if it were there, or down at your notes. Again, this technique is not optimal; it's simply a survival tactic.

Before the talk, focus on the audience.

One surprisingly effective technique to help with nerves just before the event is to focus on individual members of the audience. Really look at them, their hair, eyes, chins, makeup—everything about them. Tell yourself, "That person isn't scary. I could easily say what I have to say to him or her." If you do this with enough concentration, you will forget about being nervous, and you will have begun the all-important task of connecting with your audience. They will be familiar when you start to talk to them. You can use this technique to an even greater degree if you have a chance to mingle with the audience before the talk. Get to know them. Most of us are more comfortable talking to someone we know than to strangers.

In rehearsal, practice taking the time at the beginning, as you are starting, to "locate" the people you've identified in the audience who are familiar to you. Imagine yourself looking at them one at a time, smiling confidently, and beginning your speech. Then remember to do that when you give the speech.

Redefine your symptoms for what they are: excitement.

Those butterflies in the stomach beforehand are a sign that adrenaline is kicking in, and adrenaline helps you talk with more energy, stand straighter, react faster, think more clearly, project more personality, and fill the room more completely. So don't say to yourself, "I feel symptoms of nerves—my stomach is upset, my voice is quavering, my knees are shaking, I'm sweating, and I'm about to throw up." Instead say, "I'm excited. I can feel the anticipation. My energy level is rising. I'm going to knock 'em dead!"

Remember

There are a variety of steps you can take to help with speech anxiety. Use them depending on your level of need:

- Do your homework. The more you know about the subject, the more comfortable you will feel.

- Try writing out the speech in its entirety before your rehearsal.

- Visualize yourself being successful.

- For the truly nervous, don't visualize; begin by breathing.

- Practice your presence.

- For the terror-stricken, don't make eye contact.

- For everyone else, make real eye contact.

- Before the talk, focus on the audience.

- Redefine your symptoms for what they are: excitement.

CHAPTER 14

Get Technical

'M GOING TO CLOSE OUT THIS SECTION ON rehearsal with some comments on the technical aspects of voice production and body movement. This section is for those who like to have everything spelled out, and who can follow specific bits of advice in the heat of battle. A little self-knowledge is important here. One of my long-term clients is a very accomplished speaker who has grappled for years with his fundamentally adversarial relationship to the audience. He calls me the "touchy-feely" coach, an appellation I'm proud to accept, because I'm always telling him that if he can align himself with his audience—make friends with them, in effect—he'll achieve better results in the end. But he persists in seeing a speech as a contest. He tests the audience constantly, like an impatient professor. If he perceives that the audience is as smart as he is, then he'll agree to continue talking to it. If the audience fails him, he'll get impatient or even angry at the quality of the questions and answers.

I've coached him on some of the specific techniques he could use to warm up his body language, since we've agreed he won't change his attitude. But he reports that he's unable to monitor his body language that precisely in the heat of battle with the audience.

That's the danger of the advice that follows. I peel away the onion of behavior, in effect. You have to put the onion back together, and it takes a very self-possessed speaker to do that in the moment. It's better to work from your passion, and simply allow the expressiveness of your body to follow your feeling naturally. The alternative is called acting, and it's very difficult to do well—which is why most actors don't attempt it. Instead, they work on feeling the appropriate feelings in the moment so that their body language follows.

With that caveat, here's how to program yourself for public speaking. I'll cover voice, gesture, posture, and motion.

There's a famous, seminal study by Albert Mehrabian, one of the early researchers in communications, that sought to determine what percentage of how we decode people's communication attitudes comes from the voice, the content, or the face—the visual. The formula Mehrabian worked out indicated that 7 percent of the attitude clues came from the content, 38 percent from the tone of voice, and 55 percent from the face, its expressions and looks.

This study is often misrepresented to mean that "only 7 percent of the impact of what you say comes from the content. The rest is tone of voice and visual impact. So it doesn't really matter what you say. It's how you look that counts." This is a gross distortion of a small study that was run once and has not been replicated consistently. The most that one can say is something like the following: "When people are decoding a speaker's attitude toward the words he or she is saying, a good deal of the *implied emotional undercurrent* comes from the tone of voice and the facial expressions the speaker uses."

In general, a better way to think about this study and many others that have followed it is that getting content across memorably is difficult. Audiences don't remember much of what they hear. And they are easily distracted by visual and vocal cues. So make sure that your visual and vocal cues *reinforce your content rather than undercut it*. What follows will give you very specific advice about how to control all those visual and vocal cues you are giving out, and how to make them support your message rather than contradict it.

The voice conveys charm—or not.

Good voices have two essential qualities: presence and resonance. If you have a reasonably pleasant-sounding voice, then some basic work on breathing may be enough for you. After all, the competition is not terribly tough. But if some honest friend has told you that your voice needs work, then get yourself a good voice coach. In the meantime, read the following. Understand that what follows is only a quick primer. Whole books have been written on the voice, and you should refer to one of those if you need more work than is suggested here.

Presence is the quality that causes your voice to stand out, to be heard, to be clear and compelling. It is accomplished by bringing your voice forward into what voice experts call "the mask of your face." What is that? It's essentially ensuring that your voice is not swallowed in your throat, but rather sounds and buzzes throughout your sinuses and facial cavities.

Here's a simple test. Put your hands on your face, around your nose, and hum loudly. If you feel strong vibrations throughout your nasal area, then you're on the way to having presence.

Some people have a very hard time understanding the idea of moving your voice around in your head. If you've taken a foreign language, this concept may not be so difficult. French, for instance, is a language that is sounded in the front of the mouth, largely, with the lips. Your French teacher, if you had one, made you purse your lips unnaturally and say something like "eww" in order to capture the French "u" sound as in the second person singular *tu*. That's bringing the sound forward. Many English speakers form their sounds further back in the throat. The result can be muddy and inarticulate.

To practice bringing the sound forward into the mask of your face, try humming vowel sounds, a sort of honking, making an unnaturally nasal sound, and then keep the liveliness that this horrid sound creates when you drop back to talk naturally. The research shows that the one voice that people consistently find annoying is a nasal one, so don't overdo this exercise. Use it solely to practice bringing your voice forward to the mask of your face, so that it can resonate within your nasal passages. But couple it with hard work on resonance so that your voice still has an attractive as well as a clear sound.

Resonance is the quality that makes your voice sound rich, deep, and pleasant. In some ways, it can seem like the opposite of presence. The trick is to maximize both.

You achieve resonance by proper breathing and by talking at the right pitch.

Breathing correctly comes easily to singers who have been properly trained. The rest of us must learn to do the following. Imagine your body is an eye dropper, with the bulb in the stomach area. Breathing *in* air involves expanding the stomach, using the diaphragmatic muscles, and breathing *out* involves squeezing the diaphragm, forcing the air up and out the mouth, producing sound, like a wind instrument—or an eye dropper. If you're doing this correctly, your shoulders should not rise during either part of the breath cycle. And yes, it will make you look fat, something that is anathema in most circles. My suggestion is that you take a deep breath before you get up to speak, when your stomach is hidden by a table, if it really bothers you. If you're not willing to breathe properly, I can't help you talk well.

Once you've learned to breathe, then you've got to learn to relax everything else involved in voice production except your diaphragm. Try breathing properly, and forcing the air out of your mouth while saying "ahhhh." Now, do it again with your jaw dropped onto your chest, as relaxed as possible. Breathe, relax, and say "ahhhh." Use the relaxation exercises in chapter 11 to relax the face and throat as much as possible. Breathe in, and make big vowel sounds while you're breathing out. That's how to develop resonance. The key is to involve your whole air production capacity, not just your shoulders, as most people who breathe badly do.

The right pitch is easily determined. Figure your vocal range, which for most people is about two octaves on a keyboard. Divide the number of white notes by four, and come up a fourth of the way from the bottom end of your range. That's your natural resonance point. You should be talking at that pitch when you're just talking—most of the time. Of course, variety makes a voice interesting, so you want to regularly go above and below that point for emphasis, but you should always return to it.

I've worked with a number of clients whose voice shoots up alarmingly when adrenaline courses through their systems because of the nerves associated with public speaking. The only cure for this is to pay strict attention to your breathing. Pause before you start, breathe, swallow, and then begin. As you prepare and rehearse adequately, and have successful speaking outings, you will gain confidence, and the adrenaline problem will gradually go away.

Once you've got the basics of production down, work on variety of speed, pacing, pitch, and tone. And develop what we in the speaking business call the authoritative arc. The authoritative arc is what a strong voice does in a phrase, sentence, or thought. It starts at its natural resonance pitch. As the point is developed, the voice rises in pitch. By the end of the point, the voice returns to the natural resonance pitch. It's the opposite of asking a question, where the voice rises at the end of the sentence.

There is a curious speech quirk most widespread among the young? Where everything they say sounds like a question? Because their voices rise insistently at the end of every phrase? This is deadly in public speaking. It makes the listener nervous, uncomfortable, and uncertain as to whether the speaker knows what he or she is talking about. It also simply muddies the informational waters, because listeners are getting two messages: The content is factual, delivering information, but the tone of voice is implying a question. That's confusing. Don't do it.

By all means, do ask questions when you mean to. Questions are good, because they invite response from the audience, even if it's only thinking about the answer. Unless you're one of those annoying people who speak in questions, the variety will be welcome. You should look for all sorts of appropriate ways to vary pitch, tone, speed, volume, and all the other variables at your command. If you tend to speak in a monotone, try listening to some great speakers and imitating them. Actors, a few politicians, and some public figures like Martin Luther King, Jr., are great examples.

They have naturally wonderful voices in the same way that peerless athletes have wonderful swings, or fastballs, or whatever—they work at it.

The face conveys _and the voice_ meaning.

We bond with faces from the cradle, so the expressions a face conveys are the first place we look to decode the emotional content of a communication. And the emotional content is extremely important. Listeners are quickly overwhelmed by the amount of information a typical speech throws at them. They look to the emotional subtext to let them know what's really important. Is the speaker passionate at this point? Is she telling you by her expression that what she's saying is only somewhat important? Is the story she's narrating to be taken with a grain of salt? These sorts of clues are desperately important for the audience, and most of them are conveyed, at least in part, through the face, _and the voice._

But once again, adrenaline can be your enemy. If you've got the fight-or-flight feeling raging through your system, your face may well be expressionless. It takes a lot of muscles to make the face go, and that takes energy. You're saving that energy for the woolly mammoth.

Here's what you need to achieve anyway in spite of your adrenaline. There are a handful of expressions that are recognizable all over the world—even by primates. Some are positive, and some are negative. They are all extremely powerful ways to get meaning across. You know them in your bones, most of them. Some of them you do without even being aware that you do them.

Let's get two easy ones out of the way: the smile and the nod. Both instantly convey positive messages to the audience. You don't want to smile inappropriately, but the studies show that smiling people are generally taken to be more likeable and more attractive, so you'd be crazy not to crack a smile whenever you can.

Nodding has an even more powerful, twofold effect on your audience. First of all, it's a good way to check to see if your audience is with you. If you nod, all the nodders in the audience will nod back, especially if you make eye contact with them at the same time. People who nod back easily and readily are with you. People who keep their heads still may not be. (But remember that body language is always multidetermined. A non-nodder may just have a stiff neck or an uncomfortable chair.)

Not only that, but because the nod is so powerful, people want to be agreeable and nod back. When they do, they think like this: "Oh, I just nodded at the speaker. That must mean I agree with her. If I agree with her, she must be all right." See why nodding is a good thing? You just have to figure out a way to do it that doesn't make you look like one of those dolls with its head on a spring.

Or you could mimic Paul McCartney. He has the knack of nodding and smiling at the same time, which accounts in part for his always being the most popular of the Fab Four. Watch the video

of the *Ed Sullivan Show* from the early 1960s—or any other performance—and you'll see what I mean.

Actually, Paul has even more talent than that. He simultaneously carries out two other positive facial expressions, ones that
most people are not as consciously aware of as they are of nodding
and smiling. So Paul is firing on four cylinders at once, and for a
certain generation, that was enough positive vibes to knock 'em
dead every time—at least the girls, who were even reported occasionally to have orgasms while Paul was nodding, smiling, raising his eyebrows, and opening his eyes wide all at the same time.

Raising your eyebrows is a largely unconscious gesture that indicates openness and receptiveness and invites response. Teachers
use it when asking questions of an inert group of students. Thus,
it brings the audience in and invites it to respond. Even if your
listeners are not responding verbally, the energy level is raised
and the audience becomes more attentive.

Similarly, opening your eyes wide indicates interest. It's standard behavior in the flirting dance that goes on between mutually
attracted humans. It's even been observed in primates, so don't
practice your open-eyed behavior near a monkey cage. The caveat
with this behavior is that there are many speaking occasions
where flirtatious behavior is neither advisable nor welcome. Use
this gesture with caution. Again, all body language is multidetermined, so "interest" doesn't necessarily mean "flirtatious interest," but be conscious of whom you're opening your eyes wide at!

Now, the opposites of each of these facial gestures are just as
powerful as the positive versions. Frowning, shaking your head,
bringing your eyebrows down, and narrowing your eyes all have
various meanings appropriate for various occasions. I mention the
positive expressions first because your main objective as a speaker
is usually (but not always) to establish a positive relationship
with your audience.

Indeed, the main message you should take away from this section is that you want to have a whole range of facial gestures to

draw upon because they are so effective in conveying extra-linguistic meaning. Audiences crave them—they are interesting, and they are meaningful. So have yourself videotaped, and look to see if you can expand your repertoire of facial expressions even under conditions of adrenaline.

Gesture is for connecting with your audience.

Now we finally get to the age-old question, the one I have probably been asked by more nervous speakers who have just seen themselves on videotape than any other: What do I do with my hands?

Once again, I'm going to tell you, specifically, what you can do with your hands, but remember that self-consciousness is not the best method of achieving great results with an audience. The best method is almost always passion. When you're passionate, your hands will take care of themselves.

That said, you still need to know if you're a "windmiller," someone who learned somewhere to talk with your hands, so much that those hands become a sideshow that detracts from the message.

What are the other common mistakes? Self-defensive postures, such as the "fig leaf" posture, most commonly used by men, especially sports heroes, who are prone to placing their hands in front of their genitals and leaving them there long enough to make the rest of us wonder what they're trying to protect or hide. Hands in the pockets, hands behind the back, hands clasped rigidly in front of your chest, arms folded—all of these are completely natural, self-protective gestures. It is completely understandable, too, that a speaker would want to adopt one of those gestures, or find them comfortable. He's nervous! It feels good to protect yourself when you're nervous.

The problem is that you look defensive to the audience. Now, most audiences are willing to grant you a modest amount of self-protection, because they understand the nerves. But they also expect you to get over them after the first few minutes, and to open up as the talk progresses. Failure to do just that will eventually begin to turn the audience off, because it wants you to have something you care about enough to risk telling the audience all about it.

And you're also missing out on the positive chance of being open from the start. Such openness has an electric effect on the audience. Energy flows between speaker and listeners. They are thrilled at the unexpected openness and reward it handsomely with approval and enthusiasm.

So instead of self-defense, risk everything! Open your arms, make your gestures wide enough to include the entire audience in your "embrace," and use your hands and arms to reach toward the audience, with your palms showing. This last gesture builds trust, for reasons which probably go back a long way to primitive humanity. When you met strangers, you wanted to know if they were concealing weapons—it's where the handshake apparently came from. An open palm conveys openness and builds trust.

I often begin talks on public speaking by standing in front of the audience for five or ten minutes with my hands out to my sides, palms up. Later on in the talk, when I get to the gestures, I ask the assembled people if they can remember my gesture from the opening of the talk. No one has ever managed it. For one thing, I hold my hands still, and while that may feel uncomfortable for the speaker, it simply becomes "background" for the audience, because it looks first at motion. Thus the gesture goes straight to the unconscious mind of the audience and reassures it that I'm a trustworthy, open, nice kind of guy. Works every time. As Bob Hope or somebody is supposed to have said, "If you can fake sincerity, you've got it made."

As for the rest, if you're still uncertain about what to do with your hands, try this simple technique. Begin talking with your hands relaxed at your sides. Leave them alone. Eventually, somewhere in your talk, you'll find them creeping up above your waist to make a point. Let them! What you're doing is probably good, natural gesturing.

On the whole, avoid touching your face, head, and hair. Many speakers—both male and female—indulge in a good deal of nervous grooming while presenting. Unfortunately, grooming is also the way that the flirtation signaling begins. What happens then is that people in the audience who find you attractive may unconsciously start to think along the lines of flirtation instead of the serious subject you were hoping to impress them with. I have coached many women who have learned to their detriment that unconscious grooming in front of an executive team or board can cause those often male-dominated groups to not take them seriously. Whether you're male or female, it's best to finish your grooming in the bathroom before you speak.

I also coach people who want to know what to do with their hands not to place them below the waist. Almost all the destinations there are either unattractive or sexual. Or unattractively sexual! With the exception I noted above, where a speaker starts with hands at sides, avoid these places.

You've still got plenty of scope for gestures big and small between neck and waist, with arms open wide to your audience and hands reaching toward the people out there who want to connect with you.

One final point: Simple gestures are better, and fewer simpler gestures are better still. I mentioned the "windmill" effect earlier. If your hands are still, they are not a distraction. If they're moving, they are "information" to the audience, so they'd better support your message, or else they are detracting from it. Try to use fewer, simpler gestures at meaningful moments to underscore the meaning of what you're saying. That will help your audience understand you and retain your message. And that's what the point of the whole exercise is, after all.

And by the way, if during the course of a sixty- or ninety-minute talk you find yourself briefly sticking your hands in your pockets or crossing your arms, don't worry. The point is to be mostly open. There's no reason to be rigid about these things. People are forgiving and understanding, and audiences want you to succeed. If you've got a good relationship with the people in front of you, the last thing you need to worry about is what you're doing with your hands. Concentrate on getting your message across.

The only exception to that is the moment when you ask for questions, to begin the infamous Q&A session. I've seen many an accomplished speaker cross his arms at that point, instantly sending out the message that "I'm fine when I'm talking, but I get defensive when I allow you to talk." Don't do it!

A good posture is hard to find.

Good posture is important because it conveys energy. There's a study that speech coaches often mention that found that audiences make up their minds about speakers in the first thirty seconds of a talk. Obviously, then, it's not the soul of the speaker that's being judged. The visual impact of the presenter is crucial at first. And posture is an important part of that visual impact. If the speaker is slumped, that conveys a message of low energy. If the speaker instead bounds onto the stage, head up and shoulders back, you're going to think at least that she's alive and ready to go.

Actors often talk about three possible postures, and it's as good a way as any to think about the problem.

The first is the head posture, where, viewed from the side, the part of the body that's foremost is, in fact, the head. This is the posture of the intellectual, and it's familiar to most of us as the "professor" posture—classically, the absent-minded variety. This posture can be effective if you're trying to dominate the audience with the power of your intellect.

The second is the pelvic posture, where you lead with your hips. This posture is also known as the "Elvis" posture. It's great for lovers and rock stars, but not for serious public speakers. And yet many people stand this way unconsciously. Most teenagers do. Find a close friend and ask him or her to check you out from the side. If your hips are forward, you need to fix it.

The third posture involves a straight spine and relaxed shoulders, with the chest foremost toward the audience. You might think of it as standing the way a soldier does, only without the tension. Imagine yourself suspended from a string connected to the top of your head so that your back is upright, but most of the rest of you is fluid, not rigid. This posture is the "heart" posture, and is best for leading characters and speakers. It conveys openness and trust to the audience. Unless you're speaking to a predominately intellectual audience, try to adopt the heart posture. It's also good for your back.

Motion is either meaningful and helpful, or meaningful and confusing.

Motion is the most ignored and least effectively used aspect of nonverbal communication in public speaking. Think of your body as a large punctuation mark. What you do with it *will convey meaning,* whether you do intelligent things with it or not. I despair sometimes when watching reasonably good speakers who have prepared decent talks dance their goodwill away, moving randomly around the speaking area and conveying with their feet what they have worked so hard to overcome everywhere else—nervousness and thoughtlessness.

Voice, the face, gesture, posture—all these are important to audiences for decoding the messages you are trying to convey. But motion is the most important of all. It's the blunt instrument of public speaking. When you move toward someone, you get her attention, and you raise the energy quotient between you. If you move within four feet, as I've noted elsewhere, you've got her personal attention. If you close to less than eighteen inches in most Western countries, you've threatened her intimate boundaries. Nothing you say at that point will have any meaning for that person; she will simply be reacting to the boundary violation.

Thus, motion and the space between people is freighted with significance. If you don't think it through, and simply leave your choreography to chance, as most people do, you will send out one message in your talk and another with your body. That's confusing to the audience.

Instead, move toward the audience when you want to emphasize a point, and away when you don't. It's that simple. Move into an audience member's personal space (eighteen inches to four feet) when you want to emphasize one of the key points of your talk. Stay in social space (four feet to twelve feet) for the rest of the talk. Use public space (twelve feet or more) for large audiences and for marking pauses and shifts of topic during your presentation.

Remember that the most powerful way to use the space between you and the audience is to pick proxies in representative places throughout the audience and regularly move to the personal space of the proxies. This motion will have the effect of making the entire audience believe it has had personal contact with you.

What do you do if you're trapped on a stage and you can't get close to the audience? Use the space you have to get as close as possible to the various sections of the audience. Bill Clinton illustrated how motion works even in this limited scope during a debate with the first President Bush during the 1992 campaign. In answering a question from a member of the audience who was in the back row, Clinton moved to the very edge of the stage, with his toes hanging over, and made eye contact as only Clinton could while he spoke. Bush, in contrast, came out a little way from the chairs area and headed back to the chairs even before he was done speaking. The difference in the sense of emotional connection with the audience was profound, and indeed, Clinton's numbers started moving past Bush's after that debate.

What do you do if you're trapped behind a podium and you can't get out? Remember Elizabeth Dole, who in 1996 spoke at the Republican convention on behalf of her husband, Bob Dole, in his quest for the presidency? She began behind the podium like every other political speaker, but then she did something extraordinary. She grabbed the microphone and *left the podium and the stage* to wade into the audience. She even hugged preselected members of the audience. You can't get much more intimate than that (they were friends of hers, so it was OK). The effect on the audience in the hall was electric, and talk about Elizabeth Dole's own candidacy for president began after that night.

Interestingly, the effect was less powerful on television. Why? Because we already felt that we were in her personal space, thanks to the framing effect of the television close-up. It was the live audience for whom that gesture was effective—and it was extraordinarily effective. It was the best bit of political theater since the handshake between Arafat and Rabin, or Khrushchev pounding his shoe on the table at the United Nations.

Motion is an essential part of the theater of public speaking. If you fail to use it effectively, you cannot possibly realize your full potential as a presenter.

Rehearsal is where it gets real—but not too real.

In spite of everything I've told you in this section on rehearsal, you may still be tempted to avoid it. There's the fear, the embarrassment, and the awkwardness of pretending to do something. But it's far better to suffer those minor problems than to launch into an important speech only to discover that you can't read your notes under the bright lights, or you're thrown by the presence of audience members in places you didn't expect because you didn't see the seating arrangement beforehand, or you realize that you don't know how to make a transition from slide eight to slide nine, or you suddenly decide your conclusion doesn't make any sense.

Or even if you avoid these pitfalls and get through your speech without serious incident, you're still aware that you're leaving a good deal of potential behind in the green room. There's so much more you could have done. Many times I've had people tell me afterward that they forgot a section or felt they had to rush through a conclusion, or didn't say the most important thing. These are the comments of underrehearsed speakers.

What a waste. The only reason to give a speech is to change the world. Reach for it. Don't settle for changing it just a little, and then wishing you'd had the guts to go for broke. These are moments, when you have an audience in front of you, that you never, ever get back. Don't squander them. Make the most of them. Rehearse.

Remember

- Use the insights of modern communications research to build a public persona that communicates well with your audience.

- The voice needs both resonance and presence.

- You should speak at your natural pitch, neither too high nor too low.

- Use universally understood facial gestures to convey emotional meaning and engage the audience.

- Use open body language to connect with your audience.

- Employ the "heart" posture.

- Use the passion you feel about your subject to get your message across effectively.

PART IV

Stand and Deliver

CHAPTER 15

The Audience-Centered Speech

T'S 6:00 A.M. YOU AWAKE TO A GNAWING feeling in the pit of your stomach. For a moment you lie there in the hotel room, reconnecting, remembering where you are. Then it comes rushing back—the reason for that feeling in your stomach. Today's the day. You have a presentation to give. It's your biggest audience yet. Your successes up to this point have led to invitations to speak at more and more prestigious occasions, and today you're talking to industry leaders gathered at an exclusive conference—by invitation only. The organizers tell you there could be as many as five hundred people in the room. You can't afford to screw up now.

What thoughts run through your mind? Most people find these preshow jitters distinctly unpleasant, and they won't be happy again until the speech is history and they're relaxing with a drink in the bar. Some people fare worse; they are so debilitated by fear that if they ever get this far, they're probably vomiting in the sink by now.

A lucky few actually enjoy the experience, using the butterflies to bring them to peak performance during the presentation and reveling in the excitement of working with a receptive audience. What separates them from the others? How can *you* get there? And what are the other tricks that will help you give your best presentation ever the next time you're up?

You can begin right there in the hotel room. You need to focus on both sides of the adrenaline equation from the beginning, and now is the time to do it. Both your mind and your body are involved in creating the circle—either vicious or virtuous—that creates adrenaline, and both need to be involved in controlling and channeling it.

Great presentations combine speaker, message, and audience in a unique event.

So start by creating a picture of yourself giving a splendid speech. Make it as detailed as you can. Replay it a couple of times in your mind, until it's clear and precise. You cannot possibly do this exercise well if you haven't visited the venue and, at the very least, stood in the space you will occupy later today, imagining yourself speaking to a packed house. So I'm going to assume you've already done that. Ideally, you've already rehearsed the speech in the space, so you've got some good, specific sensory memories to draw upon.

Then, once the virtuous circle of positive thinking is initiated, treat the body just as well. Breathe properly and undertake a mild workout, especially using muscles that you know tend to tense up for you. The idea is not to exhaust yourself; that would be counterproductive. Rather, keep yourself from getting too agitated because of the unusual amounts of energy your adrenaline is providing you. If you're stuck for ideas, simply flexing and relaxing your major muscle groups should help. A brisk walk is also a good idea; spend the time going through the presentation in your mind, successfully, of course.

The truly ambitious will want to develop a good lifetime habit of warming up the voice every morning, or at the very least before each presentation. The best warm-up is the one singers use. If you're not a singer, then find a few songs that you're fond of and that are comfortably in your range, and warm up in the shower or the hotel room by breathing carefully and singing those favorite songs gently with lots of breath control and sustained pitches. Try to pick upbeat, cheerful songs. If you're agile and choose danceable songs, they can become the basis of your exercise routine as well.

Do I need to say that smoking and drinking are hard on your voice, and that you should avoid them, especially before a presentation? Water, of course, is the preferred drink of speakers. Everything else is second best or worse.

Are you feeling nervous? A little nervousness, as we've noted, is actually a good thing. Too much is debilitating. The positive imagery should help. Just invoke that every time the nerves flare up. Also, this is a good time to review the speech once again. Don't give the whole thing; it's too late for that and will only make you stale. Instead, go through the outline of the talk in your mind, so that you know exactly where you're going and what you're covering at every step of the way.

Visit the site early.

Once you've warmed up and performed the mental and physical gymnastics it takes to get yourself in peak form, go to the room (preferably before the crowds are there). If you do get to the space early enough, and there is no one or only the technical people in the room, do the "whole room" exercise that you may have undertaken during an earlier rehearsal and that I described briefly in chapter 11. It will increase your confidence and connection with the audience remarkably.

Begin at the front of the room, where you'll start talking. Take a deep breath and look around. Focus on the three walls to the left and right and in front of you. How far away are they? How tall are they? How are they lit? Can you see clearly, or does a twilight gloom invade the corners?

Now look behind you. How close is the back wall? What's on it? Anything that could possibly distract an audience? Anything that looks more interesting than you? Anything that you could trip over when you leap spasmodically backward in your nervousness?

Fix the room in your memory, its height, lighting, size, distant boundaries—the works. Then walk it. Walk the entire perimeter, stopping regularly to look back at where you began. How far away is that speaker? How hard is it to see where you'll be? Anything blocking the audience's line of sight?

The idea is to get a sense of how large the room is, and thus how hard you have to work to reach everyone in the audience. Most speakers talk to the front few rows. They have neither the volume nor the energy to reach the folks in the back. And guess what? Often those folks sit in the back because they're not terribly interested in your talk, or they're hoping to leave early, or they're related to your estranged aunt and they're there to heckle. Thus you have to try doubly hard to reach them. If you lack the necessary energy to overshoot the people farthest away, in fact, you'll never hold them.

I recently saw Michael Hammer, coauthor of *Reengineering the Corporation: A Manifesto for Business Revolution,* take the podium to make remarks after several other speakers had had their say. Each one of them had dutifully leaned into the microphone and spoken. But Hammer electrified the crowd with a simple trick: He eschewed the podium and stood at the edge of the stage, and, taking a deep breath, he bellowed his comments in a voice loud enough for all to hear comfortably. The move ensured that everyone paid attention to what he had to say, and the feeling of connection was much more powerful between Hammer and the audience than anyone else. The other speakers, before and after him, looked anemic by comparison.

Hammer, you see, knew exactly how big the room was and how much he had to project to reach the distant corners of the space. You need to know the same, whether you're miked or not. It's a matter of projecting to the farthest space so that everyone feels included. If you're smaller than the room, you begin by eliminating the back third of the audience from serious consideration of what you have to say. Why do it?

That's all you need to do. Just circle the room, imagine yourself projecting to everyone, and picture yourself succeeding. Then you can get out of there and go do something else until it's time for you to be center stage. It's good if what you're doing to fill up the time is sufficiently distracting but not terribly important, so that you're diverted but you don't have to pay much attention to the activity. You're not going to be fully present anyway, so don't expect too much from yourself. That need for nonengaging distractions is why green rooms and dressing rooms were invented.

If you have a lot more time to kill, look over your speech or give the opening a quick rehearsal. Then get out of the space and go for a walk. Or do something different that you enjoy and that will distract you. At this point of the run-up to a presentation, you're in adrenaline mode, and you're not going to be taking much in, so more rehearsal is of little use. Go to a movie.

You're almost ready to speak.

So you're back from your movie or your haircut or whatever you've done to pass the time. Now it's time to let the adrenaline be helpful to you. But you need to know the tricks of the trade.

Adrenaline can throw you off or it can carry you through your talk. Avoid the downside. Focus on the positive. Just as little unexpected problems encountered at the beginning of a presentation can throw you off your stride, three simple steps you can take before you start can help ensure that your speech gets off to a great start.

Talk to someone in the audience before you begin.

You can usually arrange to meet members of the audience before a speech, whether at a cocktail party the night before or even in the few minutes before a presentation is due to start. As you're making conversation, ask them what's on their minds, and what their needs are. Set up a question for the Q&A, if you're allowing for that. Then, when you get up to speak, imagine you're talking to that one individual. For many speakers, the effect is to warm up the delivery and calm down the nerves. It's easier to talk to one real person than a mass of unknowns. If the conversation was in depth and took place the night before, you might even be able to weave some of the audience's comments and concerns into your talk.

Shake the hand of the person who introduces you.

This simple little gesture will help ground you. It will help prevent some of the nervousness that we all feel at the beginning of a speech. It also presents a simple image of connection and trustworthiness to the audience, since the introducer is usually someone the audience knows. And it's the polite thing to do, if you've been given a great introduction.

Take a deep breath before you speak, then swallow, then begin.

The breath helps you build some resonance in your voice, keeping it from being squeaky or shaky. To do it right, though, you must breathe from your diaphragm, what speech coaches often call "belly breathing." Your stomach should inflate, and your shoulders should remain level. If you raise your shoulders when you breathe, you actually squeeze your lungs into a smaller space, constricting your voice. The swallow helps steady your voice. And the pause works well with the audience, to build a connection between you and it, and adds a little drama.

Maximize the first thirty seconds.

The first thirty seconds of any speech are key. You'll either make a good impression on the audience, helping them relax and believe that they're in store for an interesting time, or you'll do the opposite. It all comes down to posture and expression—it obviously doesn't depend on the audience's fully understanding the "inner you." So play it smart. If you stride in with lots of energy, smile confidently, and take charge of the space and the audience immediately, you'll be off to an excellent start. If you slump in, fidget your energy away, and talk only to the few people right in front of you, you'll make the opposite impression. Of course, it's easier to stride in confidently if the inner you is thriving and confident, so don't neglect the important work on that.

It's possible to undo an early bad impression, but it's not easy. It takes a lot of hard work.

The best way to start a speech is to get the audience involved from the very top. Get them to do something interesting. Then tell them your opening story and get to work. But if you get them going at the start, the energy you will unleash will amaze you.

The cliché in this situation is to ask for a show of hands: "Anyone from Poughkeepsie?" or some other such meaningless exchange. The better way is to engage them in something that relates to the topic. Get them to help you articulate the problem you're going to discuss, or identify some of the issues that lie behind the problem. If you're planning a lot of interactive work with the audience, start simple by getting them to introduce themselves to one another in smaller groups than the whole, and pick three issues, ideas, thoughts, theories, what have you, that will help you get started. Then, as with all audience interaction, be sure that you validate what they've done by getting them to report back to the whole group.

You don't have to get every single subgroup to report if time and the size of the audience doesn't permit; a representative sampling will do. It is essential that you solicit some reporting back, and that you take it seriously. It's also good to capture it visually in some way—a flip chart summary, for instance.

Another way to involve the audience from the start is to report to them about them. Audiences are always interested in hearing about themselves. It flatters their vanity. So do your homework, and tell them something interesting (and complimentary) about *them*. What percentage of them are CEOs? Or involved in not-for-profit work? Or have attained advanced degrees?

You can also quickly survey the audience on the subject you're discussing and then compare that to broader surveys you've done nationally or industrywide, for example.

Finally, there are any number of books full of "icebreakers" that basically involve getting the audience to do something silly or fun or even humiliating as a group bonding exercise. There's nothing wrong with most of these—I don't personally favor anything that diminishes the audience in its own eyes—but they work better if they are at least thematically related to the talk you're about to give.

What if disaster strikes?

For some reason, this is the scenario that every speaker dreads: some kind of snafu that embarrasses the person in front of the room. But the secret to rolling with every punch that comes your way is not to "own" the problem. Whatever goes wrong, simply acknowledge it and ask the audience what to do about it. If it's a matter of discovering that your fly is unzipped, you don't need the help of the audience to fix it, or shouldn't. But for everything else, including the usual gamut of equipment breakdowns, get the audience involved. And first acknowledge what's going on. As soon as you do that, it's not an embarrassment anymore. It's a challenge for the audience to help you meet.

I call this approach "acknowledging the hippopotamus in the room." As long as you don't recognize the presence of a problem, it's a huge issue for the audience to deal with. But once you do, the stigma of trying to cope in front of people who can easily see you're in trouble goes away, and you all get to be human together and try to solve the problem. It's by far the simpler and easier approach.

In chapter 16, we'll look at how to analyze the audience in real time.

Remember

- Use a variety of exercises to prepare during the morning of your talk.
- Visualize yourself succeeding.
- Visit the site early if you can.
- Get to know the space.
- Talk to someone in the audience before you begin.
- Remember, the audience wants you to succeed.
- Let the audience help you; if you run into problems, get them to help you solve them.

CHAPTER 16

Listen to Your Audience

S UCCESSFUL SPEAKERS HAVE ENOUGH presence of mind that they can monitor their audience's body language during the course of a presentation and react accordingly. The result is a dynamic presentation that treats the audience with respect, pausing when it needs to pause, moving on when it needs to move on.

This is what I mean about listening to the audience.

Most of us read body language unconsciously. When someone is fidgeting and not making eye contact, we sense that we're not enthralling that person. When an audience member greets our proposals with a frown, crossed arms, and a shake of the head, we get it—that person is not buying what we're offering.

But it's useful to develop your skills in reading body language consciously, both because you can become more precise in your ability to understand the reactions of various sections of the audience, for example, and because you can sense a change in the audience's opinion more quickly than if you leave the work to your subconscious.

Read an audience by using five continua.

You can analyze your audience's responses using five continua I have developed during my seventeen years of work on public speaking and rhetoric. Taken together, these continua sum up the various possible responses to your presentations. It is crucial to remember that all body language is multidetermined; that is, people cross their arms, say, for a multitude of reasons, only some of which may be meaningful to you. You need to look for clear patterns and establish a base level of nonverbal communication before you try to read too much into specific gestures. Indeed, unless you know the person or people involved well, it is unlikely that you can do more than note big shifts in attitude or stance. But those alone can be extremely useful. An audience's aggregate body language is usually a highly accurate indication of how it's feeling. Thus, it's worth learning to read the signs.

What, then, do you do with the knowledge? If you sense that things are going well, keep on. But never take a temperature reading for granted. I always periodically take a reading of my audience in order to use the positive energy in the room to go in a new direction. In that way, it never gets boring for them or me.

If you detect that you're losing them, or that they're closing off to you, stop what you're doing and ask them why. Raise the ante, and put the onus on them to help you out. Remember, a presentation doesn't happen unless the individuals in the audience receive it. So in a very real sense, it's up to them to make the talk a success. Let them do their work!

If you detect power issues, it's best to confront them head on. If the audience is arrogantly dismissing you, you must work hard to take control by using the most dominant body language at your disposal. This sort of situation is likely to arise in, say, a board of directors meeting where the assumed status of the group is very high relative to yours. You must snatch power back right away by confidently moving into the space of the dominant individuals, or the moment will pass, and the group will dismiss you as irrelevant or worse. It should be said that such a situation is unlikely. Why were you invited to speak in the first place? Presumably because you had something worthwhile to say. Stick to that. Be fearless.

Here, then, are the five continua. Use them as ways to focus your thinking about audience feedback. You don't need to monitor all five at once; the situation will tell you which continuum is most important. In the above-mentioned board of directors meeting, for example, you might be looking at powerful-subservient issues because those meetings are so often about power and control. Presenting to your team about third-quarter numbers, how they have not met expectations, and how everyone needs to work harder, you might look along the open-closed continuum, and then the committed-uncommitted. Let the situation and what is at stake dictate the audience reading you do.

The open-closed continuum indicates the receptiveness of your audience.

Signs of openness may include nodding, smiling, and other attentive, positive facial gestures. A seated audience will usually orient itself in your direction if it is open to you. Signs of closed behavior may include turning away from you, averted eyes, crossed arms, muttered (negative) comments to neighbors, frowning, and shaking the head. Open behavior on your part will increase the likelihood of open audience behavior—but how much your audience likes your message also matters!

The powerful-subservient continuum tests the power relationships in the room.

In general, powerful people maintain attitudes or postures that are elevated over those who are less powerful. Sometime powerful people may disengage, to let their minions do the heavy lifting. Watch for the hands clasped behind the head, coupled with a leaning back in the chair, and (sometimes) eyes wandering to the far left or right corner of the room. Those gestures taken together can indicate that the boss (or some lesser person) has checked out and is either finished with the conversation, meeting, or talk, or is leaving it to lesser beings. Clearly, this could be a sign of trust that the meeting is going well, for example, or a sign that the boss has lost interest—or both.

The engaged-disengaged continuum measures response to the speaker.

When an audience collectively disengages, it is a powerful response that few speakers ultimately fail to pick up. Squirming increases, eye contact becomes minimal, and everyone's shoulders slump down and away from the speaker. The key word is "ultimately," however; early, subtler signs of disengagement are important to respond to, because at that stage the audience can be won back. Look for changes in the faces in front of you; try nodding to selected members of the audience to see if they nod back. Approach one or two people in different parts of the audience; if they don't connect with you readily and eagerly, it's time for a change of pace. Try asking the audience a few questions, or give them something new to do.

The allied-opposed continuum signals alignment.

Allied audience members will unconsciously mimic your behavior; opposed audience members will do the opposite. Build on the allied behavior by approaching those audience members and having brief exchanges with them. You can either ignore those who are opposed (if they are few in number) or tackle them head on by engaging them in prolonged Socratic dialogue in which you give audience members a chance to argue the opposing viewpoint. This last tack is not for the inexperienced or nervous; faint-hearted speakers had better stick to their texts and not chance ad-libbing with the opposition.

The committed-uncommitted continuum tests depth of response.

Add up all the other continua, and you can tell when an audience, whether few or many, is committed to your presentation, talk, sales pitch, explanation, or juggling act. Committed people usually try to close the distance between them and you, either by shaking your hand or moving closer, or even just leaning forward slightly in their chairs. Uncommitted people will remain neutral or effect the opposite stance. When you see your audience is committed, it's time to close the sale, wrap up the pitch, or propose your unique solution to the problems you have been discussing. The audience is firmly situated in the palm of your hand—it's time to squeeze.

Q&A should be fun for both audience and speaker.

Let's take up some of the key moments and issues in audience-centered speaking. How do you handle the question-and-answer session? How else can you listen to an audience in open sessions like Q&A? What is the concept of personalization, and what are some other ways to involve the audience?

Some speakers fear Q&A, some love it. Usually for the same reason: It's mostly unscripted. That will either cause you to panic or to loosen up and enjoy yourself. I recommend the latter. Here are a few tips to make Q&A sessions more fun and successful.

First, always, always, *always* repeat the question. For some reason this tactic seems to be a hard one for speakers to learn. But there is nothing more deadly for an audience than to have to sit through the answer to a question it hasn't heard. Repeating the question also gives you an opportunity to rephrase it. You should always ask, "Is that a fair way to state your question?" or words to that effect, so that courtesy and justice are maintained. But most people will accept a subtle rephrasing of their questions, so take advantage of the opportunity to take some of the sting out of a tough question, or to simplify a complicated one. Why not make it easy for yourself, and the rest of the audience?

It's a subtle point, but one worth considering: When you're listening to a question, you are just like the rest of the audience for that moment. In other words, the questioner has taken over the role of speaker, briefly. As such, you need to be aware of that connection with the rest of the audience and to respect it. The audience is on your side; you should be on theirs. If the question is hostile or deliberately obfuscatory, the audience will be rooting for you to resolve it in a way that maintains the spirit of the day. Use that connection, however fleeting. Remember that an audience has voted with its feet by showing up at your speech and wants a successful day.

To answer a question, treat it like a brief, impromptu speech. State a headline response, like "No, I don't think that the release of radioactivity in the atmosphere is environmentally benign." Then, give your reasons, stories, and details in support of your position. Then restate your original position: "So for these reasons, I believe that the release of blah blah blah."

When you've answered the question, check with the person to see if he or she believes that you've answered it well, unless the question comes from a heckler.

That's really all there is to Q&A. You have every right to say "I don't know" in response to almost any question (except "When is

your mother's birthday?"). Audiences will not think you're stupid if you say "I don't know." It doesn't help to say it all the time,
but if you're reasonable in its use, it should bear up well. You
should feel free also to turn a question back on the audience and
ask it for help or answers.

Use the five kinds of listening.

Most of us use the first kind of listening during Q&A or any other
time, for that matter, and that's listening critically. When someone asks a question or ventures an opinion about something
we've said, we may respond by saying, "No, that's not what I
meant. I was talking about the green variety." Or we may object
to the premise of the question itself.

There's of course nothing wrong with this way of listening, but
when you're in front of an audience, it tends to become adversarial. Other kinds of listening are important for you to become pro-
ficient in, so that you and your audience can remain fundamentally
aligned, whether you're taking questions throughout your talk or
waiting until a Q&A session at the end.

Instead of judging the question, comment, or response from the
audience, try the second kind of listening, which involves simply
paraphrasing it back to the participant. The basic format goes something like this: "So, what I hear you saying is that you think that
yak milk is best served at room temperature, is that accurate?"

You should wait for an affirmative response from the audience
member. If there is further clarification to be done, get it right
before proceeding to answer the question. Don't move on until
the person says, "Yes, that's what I meant."

Beyond that, there are further levels of response that draw an
audience into a deeper connection with you if you carry them
out skillfully. With the third kind of listening, you can clarify a

question. This takes paraphrasing a step further, because you simplify the issue involved, and highlight what you think the key point is. This is most appropriate when the comment or question is long, confused, or has implications that you wish to bring to light. Undertake this exercise with caution. You don't want to be perceived by the audience to be dumbing down their priceless comments. You must get agreement on your restatement before proceeding.

Fourth, try empathy. That simply means "feeling the pain" behind the question. Often, you can match the pain in the audience with a personal story of your own, to show that you mean it when you say you understand where the audience is coming from. Here, the risk is that it will become all about you. Don't let it. If you are moved to tell personal stories, make sure that they don't overwhelm the audience's. Refer back frequently to their stories and keep yours shorter than theirs.

Finally, the most powerful way to connect with an audience by listening is to identify the emotion underlying the question or comment. For example, you might say, "I hear your comment about the change in the Little League laws, and I get the feeling you're really angry about them. Is that the case?" This technique works best in conjunction with another kind of listening, usually. So, you might paraphrase first, and then identify the emotion. That way, your response doesn't sound too simplistic.

This technique is particularly useful in emotionally charged situations, where the topic is explosive or the audience polarized. When feelings run high, it is a great relief to have them acknowledged. You will often find that you take the sting out of a hostile audience simply with this tactic alone. For many people, it is enough to have their feelings acknowledged; they don't expect you to agree with them.

The most powerful kinds of connections with audiences come about from first listening—actively—and then talking. It's that simple.

One secret of successful audience-centered speeches is personalization.

The art of audience-centered speaking really comes down to this: getting to know the audience as well as it is getting to know you. In other words, because you're the focus of attention, your returned attention is very gratifying to the audience. If you show an audience that you've taken the time to get to know it, it will return the favor many times.

Paying attention to the audience can take many forms, from the preparation you do beforehand to the constant monitoring during the talk itself, but one of the most powerful is the idea of *personalization*.

The concept of personalization plays off the psychological truism that people are most interested in themselves, and that their interest level in general is inversely proportional to the distance from their own concerns. If you research all you can, therefore, about the audience in front of you, you can tell them things about themselves that will warm up the talk for them and increase their interest.

Tailor the discussion of new tactics in insurance underwriting to the special situation in Connecticut, for example, where you're talking. Match the talk on Icelandic Myth to the heritage of your listeners. If you're not in Iceland, or Little Iceland in New York, weave in the myths from the countries represented in front of you. Or if you're giving a motivational speech about "being all you can be" to high school students, wrap your messages in hilarious high school stories you've gleaned from current teenagers. I stress current teens, because if you rely too much on your own memory, you'll start talking about sock hops and be met with discouraging blank stares from your increasingly restless audience.

Let me stress that the real work of personalization is simply this: getting to know your audience better. The better you know them, the better you will be able to put them at the center of your approach.

Involve the audience at each step of your talk.

How else can you get an audience involved in the moment of presenting? If you've followed the problem-solution format, there are specific ways I've mentioned earlier to involve the audience on the spot that work best at each stage of your presentation. Let's review them in order in the context of personalization.

First, either before or just after the opening hook, ask them to tell you their own stories—ask them who they are. This is a great way to get started, because there is no right or wrong here. Audiences hate being put on the spot and asked a question where they know there is a right or wrong answer, or when they know that the speaker has an answer in mind. It's the "guess what's in my head" phenomenon. It's uncomfortable and annoying. Don't do it, at least not very often. Asking an audience to tell you about itself avoids that problem.

Second, during the problem section of your talk, get them to help brainstorm aspects of the problem. If you make clear the usual rules of brainstorming, you should overcome the usual reluctance to take a chance and speak up in public only to be criticized. Brainstorming builds good team spirit and a sense of accomplishment, but only if you have some way of capturing the work of the participants. You need to be able to validate their input precisely because they will perceive it as personal. Woe betide anyone who breaks the rules of brainstorming and pans an idea. The audience will take that as a breach of trust.

The same brainstorming tactic works even better during the solution section. If you've successfully brought the audience along on the journey from why to how, from passive to active, from problem to solution, they will have great energy to invest in helping you solve the problem you've laid out before them.

Third, for a lively action step, ask the audience to play games. Games are also a good icebreaker at the beginning, as long as they are thematically related to your talk, and personalized as much as possible to the specific audience. Most people love a contest. Some people really love them. The important thing to remember here is that you must acknowledge winners and actually give out prizes. The prizes should neither be too good nor too cheap. Either extreme breeds resentment among various parts of the audience. Competition wakes up an audience and releases huge amounts of energy. If you begin a presentation with a competition, no matter how silly, you will get a buzz that will take you sailing through the first twenty minutes of the presentation on that alone.

Fourth, ask members of the audience to report to the group. This tactic works best in the solution and action step sections of your talk. You should only try this when you've already done something productive with them, so that they have something to report. In lieu of this method of interaction, try getting audience members to teach other members. Again, make sure they have something to teach. This method works best when you've trained the audience in some new technique or given them some new insight they can share. Then the technique strongly reinforces the learning and also releases the energy that most people feel when they switch from student to teacher, a switch from passive to active.

Finally, you might get the audience to design a response of some kind to what they've learned. Again, this method works very well during the action step to move the audience from passive to active, and strongly reinforces what they've learned.

Each of these techniques is a way of thinking categorically about the issue of getting audiences personally involved in the work of making a presentation a success. Without the audience, after all, there is no presentation. Why not get them to help you make it a success?

Use visuals with caution in an audience-centered presentation.

Are there audience-centered visuals? Is there ever a time when it's a good idea to use them? Given that in using them, you're taking the focus off yourself and putting it temporarily on something else, will they ever strengthen the bond you're trying to establish with the audience?

If you're using PowerPoint, the shocking answer is almost never. As I've said before, the kinds of slides that PowerPoint excels in producing—word slides, clip art—are almost without exception detrimental to the power of the connection you're trying to make with your audience.

But there are other kinds of visuals. The humble flip chart can involve the audience if you're using it to capture your listener's thoughts, rather than merely sketch out your own. Audiences are drawn in by that kind of feedback, and it's flattering to see your words and thoughts captured by the speaker.

Just make sure that you're capturing those ideas with some fidelity. People don't like to see their words distorted. If you rephrase, make sure you solicit and obtain the audience member's permission to do so.

And then there's video. Most corporate videos are slickly produced empty rubbish—they lack heart. But if you can infuse a little soul into your product, it can be a powerful way to connect with an audience. We've all had a lot of practice watching TV and movies. It's something we do very well, and we're very comfortable doing. So putting on a video immediately relaxes and charms your audience, assuming you push the right buttons.

Once the video is done, though, you have to work extra hard to get the audience's attention back. Plan a quick audience Q&A routine, or get the audience raising their hands in response to the video, something that quickly brings them back to the planet and to your orbit.

If you're very good with a video camera, here's an idea I've used with great success on a few occasions. To bring a conference to a bang-up close, videotape the audience throughout the days of the event. On the night before the end, you and your video team will need to spend most of the night editing the footage. But then you can close the conference with a video that actually shows the audience itself. You'll be amazed at the reaction. The spirit you will build in the room will more than make up for the sleepless night.

Drive your speech home by ending strongly.

How should you end an audience-centered speech? Not with a summary. Not with a Q&A.

The research shows we tend to remember best what we experience last. Accordingly, good presentations need to finish strong. The received wisdom in public speaking says that you end by "telling them what you've said." In fact, most speech occasions end with a Q&A session. Both of these endings are relatively weak. The repetition involved in a summary might reinforce learning, if anyone was listening. But most audience members are highly attuned to the cadences of presentations, and when they hear a summary, they check out. You've probably done it yourself: You start to (quietly) pack up your belongings. If you're at a conference, you surreptitiously check to see where you're supposed to go next. Maybe you get out your Palm and start looking over your schedule for the rest of the week.

You don't listen. In short, it's a weak ending.

What about a Q&A? It's a weak way to end, too. It's a freewheeling format. You can't control it. You have no idea whether the questions asked will be relevant or even intelligible.

So to end strongly, save a bit of your speech for the close—the best bit. End with a stirring call to action, or your favorite story that makes a compelling point. Then leave the stage with all eyes on you. And don't forget to say "thank you." It's the only way for the audience to be completely sure the speech is over.

Zen speaking means letting go of the speech.

Speakers find joy in public speaking when they realize that a speech is all about the audience, not the speaker. So turn the occasion over to the audience. Let it carry the energy. That's why they call it "giving" a speech. An audience is a collection of individual conversations you need to have. If you don't hand your speech over to them, they can't take it away with them.

These words are simple to say, but difficult to realize. Most speakers are so caught up in their own concerns and so driven to cover certain points or get a certain message across that they can't be bothered to think in more than a perfunctory way about the audience. And the irony is, of course, that there is no hope of getting your message across if that's all the energy you put into the audience. The audience must get it for you to have communicated. So let go, and give the moment to the audience. You will have a wonderful time, you will realize that presentations are up to the audience, not the speaker, and you will be set free.

So finally, here are four additional steps that will begin to take you down the road to the Zen insight by bringing you more fully into the moment of connecting with your audience.

Connect with your core beliefs.

Are you nervous? Your listeners will pick up on that by noting all the little nonverbal signals: rapid eye scanning, shifting feet, shoulders that "bob and weave," sweaty palms, nervous swallowing. All of these will suggest to the people you meet that you have something else besides what you're saying on your mind. The research suggests that people whose eyes shift a great deal are probably lying, so those listeners are right to be concerned. The way to minimize nervousness with your content is to make sure that what you're saying closely connects with ideas and beliefs that you're passionate about. The further we stray from our core beliefs, the more likely we are to telegraph uncertainty.

Tell us clearly how you feel.

You will increase your listeners' interest in what you have to say (as well as your own comfort level) if you become practiced at letting us know how you feel. Do you love the way the business is going right now, or do you hate it? What about that latest product launch? Was that fabulous, or was it a turkey? Are you excited about the pending IPO? Don't leave your listeners in any doubt about your attitude on important issues. But do it with tact. Avoid the "emotional bull in the china shop" syndrome of people who show up braying their own opinions without being willing to listen to others.

Use colorful language.

The art of good conversation has become so devalued that when we do meet someone who can express forcefully and elegantly what's on her mind, we cannot help but be impressed. We all think of clever things we wish we had said once the encounter is over; that's inevitable. The point is not to try to prepare memorable one-liners, but to be clear and strong about issues that are important to you. Successful use of "colorful language" will follow inevitably from passionate commitment to the topic at hand. Look constantly for ways to raise the verbal ante with metaphor; don't say, "it made us a little upset," but rather, "it hit us like the proverbial runaway train."

Finish your sentences and let others finish theirs.

Our conversational life has fallen victim to our fast-paced, fractured lifestyle. The result is that we rarely finish what we begin conversationally. But if our listeners become used to hearing fragments, they will give us only fragmentary attention. Train yourself to speak in brief, complete thoughts. Hear others out. The impact on how closely you're listened to will be surprisingly large.

Finally, you need to let go of yourself.

The essence of audience-centered speaking is to take the focus off yourself, the speaker, and put it on the audience. If you work hard on focusing on the moment at hand, you will take a giant step toward achieving that essential connection with the people in front of you. But you also need not to find the moment by obsessing about your own symptoms, whether they are pleasurable or frightening. Finally, as in most things, successful public speaking is about working so hard beforehand that during the speech you can let go of yourself and focus on the receiving end—the audience.

The irony I have witnessed over and over again in my years of coaching is that people who should know better avoid doing the work before a big speech because of the anxiety it brings up. As a result, they face much higher levels of anxiety during the speech itself, and correspondingly lower levels of achievement.

If, instead, you develop the content around your heartfelt passions, rehearse the presentation to find the moments of kinesthetic connection with your audience, and then deliver it with energy and a respect and concern for the audience, you will bring the audience to its feet and to action. You will change the world.

Remember

- Focus on the audience in the moment of delivery.
- Read the audience constantly for signs of how it is absorbing your message.
- Involve your audience at every step in order to make it part of the success of the occasion.
- Let go and give the speech to the audience.

CHAPTER 17

Audience-Centered Speaking for All Occasions

W E'RE ALL CALLED UPON TO undertake a variety of special communications tasks from time to time. Each one of these has special rules, perils, and opportunities. Keeping audience-centered speaking principles firmly in mind will help you get through them with élan.

Keep introductions to an elegant minimum.

An introduction is an opportunity to give a speaker a great launch by connecting the speaker with the audience in front of you. Introducers should keep that essential fact firmly in mind. It's not about you, it's about the other person and the audience. Then-Governor Bill Clinton forgot that when introducing the presidential nominee in 1988 at the Democratic National Convention, and spoke longer than the nominee. It was an enormous faux pas.

There's little excuse for an introduction to last longer than three to five minutes. It should cover the essential questions of the journalist: who, what, where, why, and when. Who is the speaker, *in relation to the audience*? What has the speaker done that makes her a fit presenter for this occasion? Where has the speaker done those things? If her accomplishments have some geographical connection to the occasion or the audience, we should know. Why is the speaker particularly suited to address this audience on this subject at this moment? And finally, when has the speaker accomplished what she's accomplished? If it's recent, good. If the accomplishments were from ancient days, we should know, and then be told why they still constitute good credentials ("Great taste never goes out of style, ladies and gentlemen!").

Arrange these questions so that you finish either on the speaker's most impressive credential or why the speaker should be speaking now, here, to us. Conclude by saying something very much like, "So please join me in welcoming the future president of the United States, Susanne Wright!" Then start the applause. Applause not only makes the speaker feel good, but also gives her valuable seconds of cover to get to the front of the room or the podium, and arrange notes or get the technology ready or the like.

Do not fail to shake the speaker's hand. It helps with nervousness. Then sit down and adopt the posture of a wonderful listener, attentive, focused, happy. Your job is done.

After-dinner speeches should be like dessert: short and sweet.

Legend has it that Ronald Reagan had a rule that after-dinner speeches should last no longer than twelve minutes. That's a good rule. The brains of your listeners are befuddled. They have eaten, and the blood has migrated to their stomachs. If the food was good, they are happy but full. If the food was bad, they are unhappy and want to go home or out for pizza. In either case, they don't want to sit and listen to you for long.

Have mercy on your audience. Never attempt anything too substantive after dinner. Especially if alcohol has been consumed, your audience is simply not up to anything more complicated than digesting.

So keep it light and keep it brief. If your conference organizers have scheduled an hour, don't listen to them. Talk for twelve minutes and ask for questions. Excuse anyone who wants to leave before you start the questions. That way, only your real groupies need stick around. The rest can get to the pizza.

If you're gifted as a humorist, go with that strength. If you're not, be even briefer. It's possible to make a serious point after dinner, but it's not easy. And it will send your audience on its way in a really gloomy mood. Are you prepared to shoulder the consequences?

Impromptu speaking begins with poise and ends with brevity.

We can all achieve the spontaneous poise and eloquence of a President Kennedy or (on the other side of the political spectrum) a William Bennett, if we keep a few simple rules in mind. Most people fall apart during impromptu speeches because they don't know when to stop. They end up undercutting a basically good point with verbal confusion or excessive qualification.

Instead of shooting yourself in the foot, begin with a headline summary of what you're trying to say. Then list reasons, support, arguments, stories—whatever you can use in support of your point. Then close with a repetition of your headline. That way, everyone, including you, will know that you've finished. At that point, turn the occasion back over to the audience, or the emcee, or the chair of the meeting.

A variation on this approach can be useful when you're dealing with a highly controversial subject. Give your headline, and then take the most important arguments against what you're saying one by one, discuss very briefly their good points, then explain what's wrong with the position in your opinion. Finally, explain your position. This ancient Greek method is known as the residues method, because once you've entertained and rejected all the other positions, the one that's left is the residue of the argument. I discussed it in detail in chapter 8. This approach has the enormous virtue of making your audience feel like its various opinions have been heard, even if you don't finally agree. The result is surprisingly reasoned debate. Much of the sting and fury goes out of the occasion. Try it sometime. It worked very well for President Bush in his speech on stem-cell research.

A good emcee aligns herself with the audience.

If you're ever called upon to host an event of some kind, you'll experience the curious pain that is involved in being at once responsible for and largely helpless to affect the quality of the experience your audience is having. To be sure, emcees can jump in and save a conference speaker who is going woefully astray, but it will usually be obvious to the audience what's going on.

Nonetheless, keeping a few basic rules in mind can help make the best of a difficult situation. First, you are the representative of the audience. Align yourself with them. It's your job to ask the question that puts the speaker back on track. If you sense that it's needed, the audience was there ten minutes ago. If there is something wrong with the lighting, say something. Once again, always acknowledge the hippopotamus in the room. If something is going wrong, the audience is worried, and it's your job to set them at ease.

You should regularly summarize, draw lessons, encourage audience members to think about (at least) and report to the group about (at most) what they're getting in the way of lessons, insights, and takeaways.

You're also the timekeeper. As the speakers get near the end of their time, stand up and move toward the front of the room—quietly. That will serve as a five-minute warning. When the speaker finally winds down, you begin the questioning, if that's what's in store, with a quick point or two (not a summary) and question of your own. Keep things moving. Keep them light. Business conferences are a form of entertainment. Never forget that simple truth.

You should also handle the housekeeping chores and all the other technical details that it takes to keep a conference on track. Solicit feedback frequently from the audience. You don't have to take it publicly; you can encourage people to come up to you on breaks and at the beginning and end of each day to bring up their concerns, their praise, and their criticisms. The key to remember is that, as far as the audience knows, you are there for them.

It helps to be a comedian, but it's not essential. You do have to be able to think on your feet. If you can't, don't allow yourself to be put in the position of emceeing anything larger than your kid's eighth birthday party. It will simply be too painful.

Handle the media with great care.

The media of television, radio, and print journalism, as they are practiced today, are such a dumbed-down, vicious form of public manipulation and misinformation that I wish I could say it was possible to avoid them altogether. But of course it isn't. This version of public speaking has pit bulls for an audience.

You have to think about the relationship you have with the press as something completely different than with an audience. The press is not your friend. It will not align with you. It is looking for a story, the more sensational the better. It does not want to be moved from why to how, from active to passive. It doesn't want to be moved. It wants to get you. If it can't get you, it wants to use you as a source. It doesn't mind doing both, serially or simultaneously.

So protect yourself. Decide in advance what you're going to say. On television, you can get thoughts out in eight- to twelve-second sound bites. The way to prepare is to hone down your message into three basic points, each one clearly and unambiguously delivered in twelve seconds. If that sounds like an appallingly brief form, it is. That's why people used to call it the idiot box, until any word with more than two syllables got too difficult to handle.

Most reporters are generalists. One minute, they're covering the opening of the baseball season. The next minute, it's fires in Idaho. And those are the intellectually sophisticated ones. So if you're an expert on nuclear fusion energy, face it, they don't have a clue about what you're talking about. And how can you get it across in three twelve-second bursts?

You can't. That's why television is such a lousy medium for anything intellectual, like news. All you can do is use colorful metaphors ("Nuclear fusion is like a bank that never runs out of money!") and hope for the best.

But it gets worse. Reporters often don't want to talk about what you want to talk about—or what they told you they wanted to talk about. Be prepared for them to ask almost anything in the way of the question, either because they have a story already written in their minds, or because they're out to get you, or because they don't know what they're talking about—or all three at once.

The only way to fight this is to "bridge" to the statement you want to make. Bridging takes a little practice; it is human nature to try to answer the question you're asked. But after you've been asked a hundred times to talk about how fusion energy can power automobiles when you came on the show to talk about achieving break-even, you'll learn to bridge.

It works something like this: "Powering automobiles is one in-teresting way to go, but what we're looking at right now is break-even." See? You acknowledge the question as worthwhile, and then politely change the subject. If you're not obviously hid-ing a criminal indictment, most reporters will take having the subject changed slightly with aplomb. After all, remember, *they often don't know what they're talking about.* It's a relief to them to be steered in the right direction.

So prepare your three sound bites, bridge, and keep your cool. Never be defensive. Never say "no comment," and never assume anything is off the record. Treat it for the form of gladiatorship that it is. Look to survive. And volunteer as little as possible.

To ace a job interview, have an agenda.

The secret of successful interviewing is to focus on accomplishing two tasks: conveying something relevant to the interviewer about yourself, and creating a bond—the beginning of trust—between you and the interviewer. How do you manage those two objec-tives in what is admittedly a high-stakes, high-stress, artificial situation? Here, audience-centered speaking will get you the job almost every time, as long as you remember that the audience is the interviewer in front of you, and not yourself. You're there to *connect,* not to show off.

Have an agenda.

All too many interviewees see an interview as a largely passive activity, answering the questions that are asked. A successful ap-plicant needs to have a prepared agenda, of no more than a few items, that he will cover in the interview, no matter what ques-tions are asked. The interview is a chance to bring your résumé to life. What are your three key accomplishments that this prospec-tive employer needs to know that will help her decide to hire you? What particular skills do you possess that will help you get this new job done? What makes you stand out from the pack of other applicants? Develop a few well-stated, articulate mini-speeches that you can easily and tactfully slip in during the interview. Practice "bridging" from the question to your "answer." You can tailor these set, prepared answers to specific job openings by doing a little research on the company before the interview and asking yourself, "What is the problem this company faces for which I am a solution?" Then tell the interviewer!

Mirror the interviewer.

Most interviewees are focused on their own nervousness. This heightened self-consciousness can lead to inadvertent errors in what they say and do. Focus instead on making the interviewer's job easier. The interviewer is trying to determine, on the basis of very incomplete evidence, whether or not you will make a good "fit" with the team or company. Many interviewees agree to anything in an effort to appear cooperative, while at the same time betraying their resistance inadvertently with their nervous body language. "Yes," they will say, "I'd be happy to move to Borneo," while crossing their arms defensively and turning slightly away from the interviewer. The interviewer may notice this behavior consciously, or she may simply have an uncomfortable sense that the interviewee is not truly enthusiastic. The result is a lack of trust, and a mediocre interview.

Instead, focus on making your body language congruent with the interviewer while honestly and forthrightly voicing your concerns and issues as they come up. In this way, you will create an atmosphere of candor with an underlying feeling of connection and trust. If the interviewer leans forward, wait a second and then lean forward yourself. If the interviewer leans back, do the same. Sit when the interviewer sits (and invites you to do the same) and stand when the interviewer stands. The idea is not to mimic the other person exactly, but rather to adopt the same general physical posture.

If you're interviewing with Bill Gates, and he starts rocking back and forth, you might not want to imitate that. Keep your mirroring within generally accepted norms of behavior.

Survive a videoconference by loving the camera.

If restricted travel has you thinking about booking a videoconference instead of hopping on a plane, understand that it's not a telephone call with pictures. It's actually quite a different genre. It's tough to do, but practice helps.

Why? Because we can't help ourselves; we associate videoconferencing with television. Think about what that means: On television, the programming may be stupid, but the production values are high. With a videoconference, those values are reversed. The content may be quite brilliant (you're one of the ones talking, after all), but the production is definitely B-grade.

Television studios invest enormous amounts of money in three areas that are still quite primitive in videoconferencing: lighting, sound, and camera angles. In videoconferencing, you've usually got overhead fluorescent lighting, which makes you look like the Undead. In addition, you sound like one of those tinny transistor radios from the 1950s, and you have one camera angle. The result to the people on the other end is unattractive, shrill, and static.

Nonetheless, it will get better as the technology improves. In the meantime, here are three things you can do to improve your performance. The idea is to help the audience at the other end by overdetermining your communication. Communicate more and harder than is usually necessary, in the following ways.

Love the camera.

Again, think about the television analogy. Emotion is captivating. Show some. Show more than you normally might in a face-to-face meeting.

Move your head.

Try turning the sound off on a news show and watch what the announcers do with their heads. They punctuate everything they say, nodding, shaking their heads, raising their eyebrows, and the like. After all, your head and shoulders are most of what the other party will see. Motion is more interesting than stasis.

Keep it short and colorful.

The videoconference "bandwidth" is much wider than the telephone; the other party has to decode not only your voice, but also all the visual cues you're sending. That's hard work, so give it to them short, simple, and conversational. Make it vivid, and then allow the other party to respond with questions or colorful statements of his or her own. Don't say how pleased you are; say, "I'm as happy as a pig in a mud puddle." It's all about making good television.

Use a teleprompter with caution.

Teleprompters used to be out of reach for all except national politicians and CEOs. Now they're virtually standard equipment in business meetings of any size or importance. Should you use one? The quick, audience-centered answer is no.

Getting to the answer that is most accurate for you, specifically, requires that you be honest about your abilities behind a podium. If you're a nervous speaker for whom presenting is a continuous nightmare from setting the date to the moment you say "thank you" and step down from the stage, then a teleprompter can be a highly useful crutch. It almost always makes weak speakers a little better. It brings your head up from the page, and forces you to move that head from left to right with some regularity as you scan the two text images in front of you. The impression the audience gets, since the teleprompter screens are transparent, is that you're looking at the crowd.

The downside of using a teleprompter, however, is that you're reading a text, word for word, and for most of us that creates a barrier between speaker and audience. Few people can read with all the life and passion that they converse. Further, using a teleprompter traps you behind the podium, another barrier between you and the audience. Unless you're a politician at a rally, with supporters looking for reasons to leap to their feet and scream their enthusiasm, it's very difficult to connect with an audience in a visceral way when you stay behind the podium and read a text.

So it's your call. If you're a confident speaker, you're better off without one, unless you're accepting your party's nomination for president. If you decide to use one, here are a few tips to make the experience better.

1. **REHEARSE.** Reading a teleprompter is not a natural human activity. Give yourself some time before the day itself to practice and get used to it. On the day itself, it's too late—you'll have too much adrenaline.

2. **LEARN FROM PRESIDENT REAGAN.** Reagan could vary the pace with which he rotated his head from side to side, thus giving the impression that he was looking at the audience spontaneously. The technique added life and interest to his performance.

3. **VARY YOUR PACE AND PITCH.** The teleprompter operator will follow you. Don't fall into a monotonous, unvarying rhythm as you read. Speed up. Slow down.

4. **HAVE A BACK-UP WRITTEN TEXT.** Occasionally it all breaks down—it happened to President Clinton during a State of the Union address. Keep a text on the podium and keep your place in it.

Moderating is an underappreciated art.

Moderating a panel is as easy as herding butterflies. Not only must moderators unite participants around a common goal, they must also provide the structure and control that enables even butterflies to fly in formation.

Is there any good reason to fill the universe with more panels? It's an important question. The best that can be said of most panels is that if you really like one of the speakers, you wish she were the only one talking. But if you hate them all, at least no single one lasts all that long. On the other hand, it's extremely difficult to remember anything said on a panel, because of the serial format usually adopted by the participants. Unless the panel gets into a real argument, the results are usually less than compelling.

But we will always have them among us, so here's how to make the best of them. Like the emcee or host, think of yourself as an advocate for the audience. It's your job to keep the panelists on track, to draw out the lessons, to pit one panelist against another to try to get an interesting and thought-provoking discussion going.

I once saw Daniel Goleman, the emotional intelligence speaker, sitting on a panel with a representative from a company that believed in annually cutting out the bottom 20 percent performing employees. Two more diametrically opposed positions could hardly be imagined. And yet, the panel nearly went the distance without these two ideas being seriously opposed. It demonstrated the extraordinary urge of panelists to agree with one another, even when they know better. Fortunately, for that particular panel, the moderator did intervene and point out that there was a real argument to be had. The result then was interesting. But left to the speakers, the audience would have been pardoned for thinking that Goleman and his adversary were largely in agreement.

It's also your job to introduce the panelists and make them follow the ground rules—whatever you establish—about who's going to talk when and for how long. It's best not to let the panelists spend too much time giving "opening remarks." Panelists love these, because they almost always give a short version of their standard speech, the one that reports on the book, or the research, or the like. This is all very well, but it means that the audience is getting the worst of all possible experiences. It's getting the short (so less thorough) version of the thinker's position. But all these talks last long enough, usually, to prevent much real discussion from happening. Which is of course why the panelists want to do precisely that. It's risky to debate in public. What if you're shown up? But that is exactly what the audience wants and deserves to see.

After all, what is the point of having a panel if it doesn't pit the competing ideas one against the other? The panel could be a wonderful chance for an audience to see which idea is stronger. In the world of business, there are thousands of competing frameworks, insights, matrices, and the like, all purporting to have the last word on strategy, or how to use IT, or how to motivate employees, or what makes a great company last—you know the drill. Which one of these ideas is best? It's hard work sorting them all out. So a panel could be a real opportunity to let a few of these ideas go head to head and see which one wins.

That's the real opportunity. But it won't happen unless the astute moderator makes it happen. So do your homework. Prepare your introductions and questions, and keep prodding those speakers. Summarize (briefly) at regular intervals. Report back to the audience about what it's learning, or ask it to report to you. You are its advocate, remember. Never get too far away from it.

At the end, try to draw a couple of lessons. Don't summarize exhaustively—no one wants it. Instead, ask the audience, or tell the audience, what a few key takeaways are. Let it go at that. This is not a perfect art form.

> **Close a big sale successfully by listening to the customer.**

The key to closing the big sale is to create trust. You create trust in your audience by solving their problems for them, not by showing off your expertise. So begin an important sales speech with questions. You need to find out what the problems are of the people in front of you before you can solve them.

Ideally, of course, you will have thoroughly researched the issues involved before you attempt to close the big sale. You will have figured out what the problems are, and how your product or service will solve those problems.

Resist the temptation to jump to the conclusion, your answer, too quickly. Audiences won't find you credible unless you spend almost as long dwelling on the problem as you do on the answer. You have to show that you not only understand, but empathize with them. You're taking your audience on a journey toward the solution you're proposing, and it's essential that you begin by showing them that you know what their problems look and feel like.

If your product or solution triggers a problem that your audience doesn't know it has—if you're selling ice to the Inuit, for example—then you have to spend correspondingly longer on the problem, establishing its credibility, and yours.

Once you've thoroughly established the problem and elicited the audience's buy-in through close questioning, then you are ready to move on to your solution.

Here, you have to resist the temptation to talk about the product or service itself. Rather, describe it in terms of what it can do for your audience. Take the infamous car salesperson. If he spends lots of your time talking about horsepower and wheel size and "what this baby can do," he's going to bore everyone except highly testosterone-charged teens.

If, on the other hand, he's spent some time finding out how many kids you have, and begins to point out how the back seat can go down to create a bed for those long car trips to Canada you told him you take every summer, that's interesting to you. If you're one of those people who can't seem to go more than ten minutes without a drink of lime-flavored mineral water, then all those cupholders are fascinating. But the salesperson first has to notice the water bottle you're clutching, and ask you about your strange compulsion to drink constantly, before he can point those cupholders out without risking your alienation.

Closing a sale requires spending some time looking at your product or service from the customer's point of view, and then telling that customer how your offer meets her needs. Successful sales pitches take imagination to prepare.

Finally, of course, you have to ask for the sale. Judge readiness by moderating your audience's body language (see chapter 16). When the time is ripe, close your presentation with a straight-forward, polite request for action on the audience's part. Make it a reasonable first step if you're uncertain about the final result— this tactic usually yields better results than asking for the moon. Get your listeners to take some small action, and they are far more likely to take the final big one you're hoping for. But don't be deceptive. It's never worth jeopardizing the relationship.

Inspire change by giving them compelling reasons to change.

How do you kick off a big change effort? Fundamentally, you have to contrast the state of things as they are now with the state of things as they might be if the change is successful, and per-suade people it's worth journeying from one to the other.

There are two ways to accomplish this difficult feat. Both in-volve focusing on your audience. You need to know the audience well enough to know how to create one of two images in its mind. First, the Burning Building Approach. Second, the Promised Land Picture. They can also be combined, but that approach takes considerable finesse and risks overloading your audience with conflicting images.

The Burning Building Approach basically describes the status quo in words so dire that only a madman or a fool would want things to continue as they are. Trust is important here, too, so don't distort the facts in order to create a false picture of terror. Those words will almost certainly come back to haunt you later when the truth emerges. Once trust with an audience is broken, it is virtually impossible to get it back.

If you've described the current situation at your company in sufficiently alarming terms, you've created a desire for change in your audience. Then you need to give that desire an outlet by enlisting its energy in designing a solution. It's extremely important that you get the audience involved at this stage. The key is to take your audience from passive recipients to active enlistees.

This stage is where most change leadership fails. Because the leader thinks it's her job to solve all the problems the company has, she spends a lot of energy in creating a solution beforehand. The result is resentment or indifference from the employees. Their thought processes run something like this. "You got me all alarmed. Now you tell me there's a way out. Why get me so worked up? You knew all along that things weren't so desperate."

Instead, you can reveal the main outlines of a plan going forward, but it is essential to leave substantial parts of the picture for the audience to fill in. Then you will take the energy you've created and channel it into getting to work on the solution. That key step alone will go a long way toward ensuring that your change program will be met with enthusiastic enlistment instead of the usual suspicion, cynicism, and indifference.

If you don't allow audiences to generate energy and then release it in action, their responses will remain those of spectators. And spectators are not what you want participating in large-scale change programs with high stakes. Failure under those conditions is almost guaranteed.

The Promised Land Picture is almost exactly the opposite of the Burning Building Approach. You begin by describing an adequate status quo. Once again, the approach has to be honest because of the risk of the backlash when the truth comes out later.

Then you deliver, in glowing terms, a picture of a future state that has so much allure for your listeners that they are unable to resist it. Is it an IPO that will make them all millionaires? That worked pretty well for the dot-coms until it became clear that the dream had died. Is it the opportunity to participate in historically great work? Is it the chance to become world famous, breaking all previous records for glory? Money, glory, and fame pretty much sum up the basic human motivations in the workplace. If you're not tapping into one of those, you're probably not going deep enough.

The key, once again, is that you have to understand what your audience wants. If you misread your people and offer them an outsized prize that they're really not interested in, you'll disgust them. Or invite ridicule.

If you've held out a sufficiently alluring prize, then you've created energy in your audience once again, energy that needs an outlet. At this point, you need to enlist your audience's aid in telling you how you're going to get to that Promised Land. If you do the work for the audience, all that energy gets dissipated and you won't enroll anyone in the cause. If they do the work, then your listeners will be ready to jump the hurdles and go around the roadblocks to get to the desired endpoint.

You can begin this work in the presentation session itself, but you don't have to complete it. It's usually better to get your listeners to work on some aspect of the path forward, rather than the whole answer. If it all can be created by one audience on the fly, then it probably isn't that difficult to achieve, and what was all the fuss about? Rather, give out assignments for work teams going forward so that the energy continues pointed in the right direction and focused on the right problems.

Persuade the board by framing the question appropriately.

Boards tend to suffer from corporate groupthink. All else being equal, they'll almost always choose the middle option, the reasonable solution, the blandest alternative. That's called exercising fiduciary responsibility. It's what boards are paid to do, essentially: Keep the corporate patient alive.

So how do you get them to take radical action? How do you persuade them to invest in the space-age widget factory when they've always been satisfied with those Model T's?

It's not easy. You can use elements of the foregoing approaches to improve your chances of success, but the needs of a board are sufficiently different from the audiences in the previous two examples that the techniques espoused there are not guaranteed to work.

Thus, you can describe a Burning Building, or a Promised Land, or you can ask the board questions in an effort to determine what it is worrying about, and then speak to those worries. But none of these approaches will necessarily motivate a board to take more than incremental steps, because it has an inherently conservative role to play.

Instead, you need to minimize the radical nature of the investment you are proposing. Of course, honesty is essential here as in the other presentations. But if you frame the step you want to take as simply one more in a logical set of steps you have been taking successfully all along, you'll allow the board to fulfill its essentially conservative mission.

Once again, you begin with questions. In this case, the questions should be designed to create the frame you wish to establish. How does the board see the nature of the competition? What are the threats to the markets we are currently selling in? What is the likelihood that a new competitor could come along and redefine the market away from our products?

Next, tell the board members a story that reproduces in miniature the big picture of opportunity you want them to see. If the opportunity has been framed within a context of marketplace threats and change, board members will be much more likely to see that opportunity as a logical next step.

Then begin to describe the need that your investment will fulfill. Again, paint the picture in terms of consistency with the board's previous actions. The company has invested in factories before. Just because this one is on the space station doesn't mean that the issues involved are hugely different! You still have to iron out wrinkles and get the plant running smoothly. It's still all about the execution, right?

Finally, frame the investment opportunity in terms of the board's long-term vision for the company. How does this step represent a logical next step on that journey from one little factory in East Bangor to world domination? How will this step consistently and logically allow the company to get to that end state the board wants?

Don't forget to ask for the sale. And if you've enlisted the aid of a few individual members of the board beforehand, that won't hurt either. The key to succeeding in tough presentations is to use the audience's energy to get them headed in the direction you want it to go, whether you're closing a big sale, inspiring change, or prompting a board to take action.

There are times when it's best not to present.

The crisis hit early on Monday morning. Over the weekend, some reporter who should have been spending more time with his kids found out about a potential recall for the hit new toy that your company has been producing as fast as it can. Wall Street responded by taking 30 percent of the stock value away in the first twenty minutes of trading. You're the marketer in charge of the toy, and it has been all milk and honey until now—the product was an instant smash and everyone has been calling you the next Toy Genius. Now your phone is ringing off the hook, and it's the press, as well as your company spokeswoman, who wants you to hold a news conference as soon as possible. The company doesn't have a crisis communication plan in place; it's something you always meant to do, but never got around to. You've had a little experience talking in public, and you're reasonably comfortable with it, but nothing substantial in front of the press. What do you do?

Leave it to the pros. In the scenario above, resist the temptation to play the hero. Knowing what to say to the press, and what not to say, is difficult under the best of circumstances. Under these conditions, you're liable to say something unintentionally disastrous. Leave it to the spokesperson, unless the recall involves injured children, in which case you'd better hope that your CEO is good in front of the press, because the top dog has to bark when kids' lives and limbs are on the line.

There's a reason why presidents and other really important folks have spokespeople. They can build a rapport with specific members of the press, as well as expertise in the fine art of knowing when to stay on message (almost always) and when to go off (hardly ever).

Beware the briefing.

Presentations are not good venues for conveying information. Whether it's to the press or internally to your company or the investor community, keep your briefings just that—brief. If you've got a lot of information to get across, hand it out in written form. People, even reporters who are trained in taking in information, rarely retain much detail. They are entirely likely to get it wrong.

Briefings are useful to establish credibility by making a few basic points about the issue or product in question and then taking a limited number of questions. Whoever the speaker is should be well briefed beforehand in the right messages and rehearsed in delivery. This is not a natural act. All the rules of engagement with the press apply. The excitement and adrenaline that goes with public speaking usually prompts a kind of hysterical relief to set in after the first few minutes, and many an inexperienced presenter has given the game away by spilling way too much information and so obscuring the key messages that the occasion was designed to broadcast.

On the other hand, avoid also the unutterably routine. Whether an internal meeting or an external one, once a regularly scheduled speaking event becomes routine, it's time to question its existence and your presence there. First of all, it's not worth the aggravation involved in cranking up the adrenaline if no one cares whether you're there or not. Presentations should be reserved for the times when the speaker, the occasion, and the audience all need to be there—when what takes place couldn't happen any other way. Use that as a simple test. Ask yourself, could we handle this routine event with e-mail, or a memo, or some other channel?

The risk is that you'll start treating the regular event as casually as everyone else, and you'll be tempted to wing it. Most people think they've been brilliant when they've winged it, but the audience usually has a different memory. Even the impromptu should be rehearsed, if it's important. And if it isn't, don't do it.

Give no presentation before its time. You will sometimes be pressured to give a presentation in a crisis before all the facts are in. Or when you're thrown off balance by some tragedy or disaster. When your emotions are running high, try to avoid the podium. You're liable to say things you'll regret later. A presentation is a performance, and while you need to have access to your emotional responses during a performance, you will not do well if you are ruled by them. You want a warm heart and a cool head when you're speaking in public. If events force a response, then keep it brief and be as responsive as you can within that particular moment. Don't guess, predict, analyze, speculate, infer, or otherwise stray from the immediate, the known, and the concrete.

To create better business conferences, tell a good story.

I've spent a good deal of my professional life at business conferences, helping the speakers, designing better break-out groups, and creating themes for the whole. My conclusion? Three things in life are certain: death, taxes, and the fact that somewhere in the world, at this very moment, people at business conferences are delivering boring presentations to roomfuls of hapless listeners who wish they were somewhere else.

What is it about the business presentation that virtually requires boredom? The fault lies not solely in the stars but also in ourselves. The expectations are so clearly set by conference organizers, audience, and speakers alike. There will be a cigar-box shaped room or an enormous ballroom. There will be the sleep-inducing roar of white noise from the air conditioning system, and barely adequate lighting. There will be a succession of monotonous speakers at the front who rarely look at, let alone connect with, the audience. There will be a succession of word-covered slides to ensure that the audience has something to look at, since few signs of life are coming from the speaker. The speaker will drone on for fifty-five minutes, or eighty-five, and then say, "Are there any questions?" These magic words signal most of the audience to prepare to leave, and a handful of hardy souls to venture a few dispirited questions.

To be sure, there are some speakers who perform well even under these conditions, and their speaking fees reflect this ability. But the great majority merely carry out the Curse of the Boring Business Presentation again and again.

Why must this lack of originality rule the day? Why don't more organizers plan for something different? Why don't more speakers offer something new? Why don't more audiences rebel?

The simple truth is that it's easy to be mediocre. And it's more difficult to offer originality in speeches and conferences. But there are ways for the brave and energetic to experiment. Begin by becoming audience-centered. Ask yourself, what is the story I want to tell to this particular audience? Become more interactive with your audiences before, during, and after the event—and the individual presentations. Personalize the experience for your audience. Include them in the planning and execution of the conference. Break each of the expectations enumerated above. Take the experience out of the cigar-shaped room or ballroom, the white noise, the dim lighting. Don't have a succession of speakers. Don't permit slides. In short, create good theater, which begins with light, sound, and story and takes us into the realm of magic—the place business presentations should inhabit, too.

SPEECHES THAT CHANGED THE WORLD

President Reagan Reassures and Heals a Nation

Anyone who was watching the broadcast remembers it with painful clarity. The space shuttle Challenger shot up from the launching pad into a cloudless sky. Cheers erupted from the control room. It looked like another perfect launch. And then, the inconceivable happened: The rocket ship exploded, killing the seven astronauts aboard and igniting the grief of a nation.

It was January 28, 1986. President Ronald Reagan was scheduled to address the nation that night on the State of the Union. Instead, his staff went into high gear when the president decided that he had to speak to an anguished people about the tragedy that had just occurred.

The result was one of the great speeches of the twentieth century. It took the form of a funeral oration, a genre famously embodied by Pericles' funeral oration from 430 B.C. in honor of the soldiers who fought and died in the Peloponnesian War and by Lincoln's Gettysburg Address. Daunting company indeed—and a genre with certain expectations. That President Reagan and his speechwriters fulfilled those expectations so well shows that they had a keen understanding of both the emotional needs of the situation and the generic expectations of the form.

Few of us are called upon to give funeral orations, but the genre is curiously similar to another form that most public speakers must use quite often: introductions. What are the requirements of the genres, and what specifically can we learn from Reagan's example?

In moments of public ritual, do not fail to follow the rules.

An introduction, just like a funeral oration, must answer certain questions about the recipient. *Who* is being introduced or honored? *What* is the nature of their contribution or sacrifice? *Why* is it important for this particular audience to hear about it? Two other questions, *when* and *where* did the speaker acquire her expertise?, are also relevant. Failure to answer these key questions sincerely and briefly will lead to resentment and confusion on the part of the audience. So cover all the bases as succinctly as possible, omitting none, and once you have, sit down. Turn the spotlight on the principal speaker of the day, if it is an introduction, or leave the grieving to nurse their wounds if it is a funeral oration.

Reagan's speech lasted only seven minutes, yet it began the healing process for a nation and reassured us all that the astronauts had not died in vain. Introductions in most business situations should be even shorter, typically three minutes or less.

Tell us who is being honored.

One of the simple, yet crucial moments of both kinds of speeches involves literally naming the person or persons involved. Introductions should conclude (and funeral orations begin) with the naming of the person in question. A typical line goes something like this: "Will you please join me in welcoming John Doe." This line always initiates applause, which gives the speaker a little cover to reach the stage, and begins the speech on a positive note.

In Reagan's case, he handled the chore elegantly and powerfully: "But they, the Challenger Seven, were aware of the dangers, overcame them, and did their jobs brilliantly. We mourn seven heroes: Michael Smith, Dick Scobee, Judith Resnik, Ronald McNair, Ellison Onizuka, Gregory Jarvis, and Christa McAuliffe. We mourn their loss as a nation together."

By calling them heroes, Reagan makes the mere list more impressive, and gives his audience formal permission to register the loss of each one and mourn them collectively.

In the case of introductions, speakers should go on to give us the relevant bits of the subject's résumé. Tell us those aspects of the presenter's career that play importantly on the subject, the occasion, and the audience at hand.

Speak directly to special groups in the audience.

Did you ever wonder why formal speeches begin with the mention-ing of any dignitaries in the audience? "President Smith, Senator Jones, Representatives X, Y, and Z, ladies and gentleman" is a generic example we have all heard many times. The purpose of the gesture is to raise the level of the discourse, creating a formality that puts all on notice that something truly public is about to take place. But Reagan takes the gesture a little further and addresses some of his comments to specific members of the national television audience to whom he is speaking. He gives special words of comfort to the families of the astronauts, and to the schoolchildren who were watching the liftoff. The purpose is to acknowledge, of course, the special pain that those groups are feeling. But it also allows the rest of us to put our grief in perspective. That is an important part of the healing process. And paradoxically, it allows us all to mourn together, because our roles have been clearly defined. We don't have to wonder, awkwardly, just how bad we should feel relative to, say, Christa McAuliffe's immedi-ate family.

By being clear about who the audience is and what their specific roles are, a good speaker can bring an audience together into a tem-porary community, greatly enhancing the power of the subsequent presentations.

The Secret of Charisma ✳✳

WHAT IS CHARISMA? IS IT A mystery, a collision between the right speaker, the right theme, the right moment, and the right audience?

It's all that and more, but it begins with you and where you put your energy.

It's time to realize that the only reason to feel nervous is to use that adrenaline to speak with more energy. Because presentations aren't about you, the speaker. They're about the audience. Good public speaking begins with respecting the audience. The moment you realize that *it's not what you say that counts in the end, but what the audience hears,* you will be on the road toward becoming a great, charismatic speaker. And you'll forget about your own nervousness.

Charisma is first of all about self-forgetfulness—the kind of self-forgetfulness that comes after self-mastery, not before. It is the self-forgetfulness of the master, not the apprentice.

How does that actually work in practice? You need to begin by shifting your focus from your own symptoms to the audience's reception of your presentation. *Concentrate on them.* Make eye contact for five to six seconds with people in the front, left and right, and the back. Watch their body language. Are they engaged? Have they checked out? If they have, stop and ask them what's on their mind—in the context of the presentation. Take their "temperature." Move in close to selected parts of the audience, as close as four feet. You'll get them back.

Most speakers use their slides as a crutch to help them limp through a lame presentation. Or as an outline for themselves because they haven't adequately prepared for the talk. Rarely are slides actually used for the purpose they are best suited to: visually reinforcing key points in a presentation. Here's a radical thought: Don't use any slides at all. You won't miss them, and the audience won't either. It will remove one barrier between you and the audience, and you will be one step closer to becoming an audience-centered speaker. Your charisma quotient will go up automatically.

All public speakers want to be charismatic. But charisma ultimately comes from having something true and heartfelt to put on the line in front of your audience. Charisma comes from the honest expression of emotion, when something real is at stake. To be a successful speaker, you have to confront yourself, perhaps for the first time, and decide who you are and what you stand for. When you are able to share that with an audience, they will stand up and cheer, because you will have forgotten about yourself and your nervousness and given something real to *them*.

There is the matter, also, of courtesy to the audience and its needs. For example, the attention span of an audience diminishes rapidly as the day goes on. By dinnertime, it's twelve minutes or

less. If called upon to give an after-dinner speech, especially if alcohol has been served, keep it to seven minutes if you can. You're
competing with the audience's gastric juices, and they always win.

Similarly, always respect the time period set aside for your
presentation. If you've agreed to speak for an hour, go for forty-
five or fifty minutes and stop for questions. Never run long. No-
body ever asked a public speaker for an encore. And don't keep
people waiting for a meal. If you're the last speaker before lunch,
end a little early. They're thinking about their salads anyhow.

Finally, don't forget to study the speeches of the charismatic
orators of our day. There is almost always an ethical dimension to
their messages. They first tell their audiences why they should
strive for some goal or attempt to accomplish some task. Then
they tell them how. And then they give their audiences something to do, either rhetorically or actually. Most great political
speeches end with either a rhetorical charge to the audience ("Ask
not what your country can do for you—ask what you can do for
your country") or a chance for the audience to chant something
back to the speaker (Jesse Jackson's "Keep hope alive"). This device moves the audience from passive to active, and helps bring
them to the cause. Give your audiences something to do, or they
will just remain passive observers.

The fastest way to kill an audience is to read to them from a
text at a podium. Both the text and the podium separate the
speaker from his listeners. Why should an audience have to work
hard to bridge the gap? But memorizing a speech so you can leave
the notes behind can be equally deadening. Unless you're an accomplished actor, you probably can't recite lines with anything
like the life they need to keep an audience engaged. Some speakers find it useful to memorize the beginning and ending of a presentation, in order to begin and end error-free, but it is better to
adopt a conversational tone throughout, speak from notes, and
practice until you're comfortable with the material.

Your listeners grant you credibility to start with. They have voted with their feet; they have come to hear you talk. Thus, initially at least, they are hoping that you will succeed. The credibility they have given you is yours to lose. Don't tell your audience too little or too much. Both tactics undermine credibility. Give your listeners enough supporting data to illustrate but not to exhaust. And make sure it is accurate.

Most people respond to a speaker who has a scapegoat for the audience's problems. But an audience will not listen for long if that is all a speaker has. Don't get up in front of a group of people to speak unless you have something positive to offer. Listeners provisionally give you their trust, that you are an authority, that you do have something to say. Like credibility, it is yours to lose. The fastest way to lose it is to have only negative messages for your audience. Listeners are looking to you for two things, primarily: to identify their problems, and to solve them. By doing both, you cement the bond of trust between you and them.

There are two secrets for great, charismatic public speaking: enjoying yourself, and telling a strong, coherent story. It is difficult to accomplish the former without having the latter. Take the time to develop a story that comes from your own thoughts and beliefs. If you're fundamentally telling someone else's tale, you'll never achieve that happy state where you and your listeners are as one, and you're all having a great time.

A presentation belongs to its listeners. If they don't get it, no communication has taken place, and everyone's time has been wasted. If they do get it, you have the chance to change the world.

ABOUT THE AUTHOR

NICK MORGAN is the founder of Public Words, a communications consulting company, and a coach to executives and organizations on a wide range of communications issues. He regularly leads seminars on communications skills for corporations, professional groups, and universities, and is an adjunct professor at Lehigh University. He is also the editor of a high-tech journal, the *CSC Research Services Journal*, and of the *Harvard Management Communication Letter*.

Previously, Morgan has taught in the English department at the University of Virginia, where he also served as Assistant Vice President and Provost. He wrote more than 100 speeches for Virginia Governor Charles S. Robb during the final two years of his term. He has worked as a senior speechwriter in a Fortune 50 corporation and written many speeches and public relations materials for corporate CEOs, educators, and political leaders. Morgan also served as the public relations director for Princeton University's fund-raising program and taught public speaking in the English department there.

Morgan received his A.B. in English literature from Princeton University and his M. A. and Ph.D. in theory and English literature from the University of Virginia. He is the author of a book on Dickens, a screenplay, five theatrical plays, and hundreds of articles for regional and national periodicals.